# Tour Through the Eastern Counties of England 1722 by Daniel Defoe

Daniel Defoe is most well-known for his classic novels *Robinson Crusoe* and *Moll Flanders*. Born around 1660, he was also a journalist, a pamphleteer, a businessman, a spy. His life was long and colourful, and the breadth of his work, still highly regarded, is infused with similar vigour.

It is said that only the bible has been printed in more languages than Robinson Crusoe. Defoe is also noted for being one of the earliest proponents of the novel. He was extremely prolific and a very versatile writer, producing several hundred books, pamphlets, and journals on various topics including politics, crime, religion, marriage, psychology and the supernatural. He was also a pioneer of economic journalism though was made bankrupt on more on one occasion and usually mired in debt.

In later life Defoe was often most seen on Sundays when bailiffs and the like could legally make no move on him. Allegedly it was whilst hiding from creditors that he died on April 24th, 1731. He was interred in Bunhill Fields, London.

## Index of Contents

INTRODUCTION
TOUR THROUGH THE EASTERN COUNTIES OF ENGLAND, 1722
A DIARY: OR, AN ACCOUNT OF THE SIEGE AND BLOCKADE OF COLCHESTER, A.D. 1648
NORFOLK
APPENDIX
DANIEL DEFOE – A SHORT INTRODUCTION
DANIEL DEFOE – A CONCISE BIBLIOGRAPHY

## INTRODUCTION

Defoe's "particular and diverting account of whatever is curious and worth observation" in his native country, told in a series of letters, was founded upon seventeen separate tours in the counties, and three larger tours through the whole country. He said he had "viewed the north part of England and the south part of Scotland five several times over," and he thought it worth while to note what he saw, because, "the fate of things gives a new face to things; produces changes in low life, and innumerable incidents; plants and supplants families; raises and sinks towns; removes manufactures and trade; great towns decay and small towns rise; new towns, new palaces, and new seats are built every day; great rivers and good harbours dry up, and grow useless; again, new ports are opened; brooks are made rivers; small rivers navigable pools, and harbours are made where there were none before, and the like." We are endeavouring, by little books published from time to time in this "National Library," to secure some record of the changes in our land and in our manners as a people, and of what was worth record in his day we can wish for no better reporter than Defoe.

Here, therefore, is Defoe's first letter, which describes a Tour through the Eastern Counties as they were in 1722. It opens his first volume, published in 1724, which was entitled, "A Tour through the whole

Island of Great Britain, Divided into Circuits or Journies. Giving a Particular and Diverting Account of whatever is Curious and worth Observation, viz., I. A Description of the Principal Cities and Towns, their Situation, Magnitude, Government, and Commerce. II. The Customs, Manners, Speech, as also the Exercises, Diversions, and Employment of the People. III. The Produce and Improvement of the Lands, the Trade and Manufactures. IV. The Sea Ports and Fortifications, the Course of Rivers, and the Inland Navigation. V. The Public Edifices, Seats and Palaces of the Nobility and Gentry. With Useful Observations upon the Whole. Particularly fitted for the Reading of such as Desire to Travel over the Island. By a Gentleman." The Second Volume of the Tour was published in June, 1725; and the Third Volume, giving a Tour through Scotland with a Map of Scotland by Mr. Moll, followed in August, 1726, completing the record of what Defoe called "a tedious and very expensive five years' Travel." However tedious the travel may have been, Defoe's account of it is anything but tedious reading.

The change of times is in this letter vividly illustrated in this volume by Defoe's account of life as he found it in the undrained Essex marshes. Life in them was so unhealthy that the land was cheap, men thus were tempted to take fevers for grazing and corn-growing. They became fairly acclimatised, but when they brought their wives in fresh and healthy from the uplands the women sickened and perished so fast, that it was common to find a man with his sixth or eighth wife, and Defoe was told of an old farmer who was living with his twenty-fifth wife, and had a son about thirty-five years old, who had been married to about fourteen wives. Custom had even dulled the sense of this horrible state of things until the frequent change of wives became a local joke.

We have also a reminder in this volume of the traces and fresh memories of Civil War in the account of the Siege of Colchester, which is a bit of realisation such as no man could give better than Defoe. We may note also the fulness of detail in his account of Ipswich, a town that he first knew as a child of seven. He tells how it was once noted for strong collier vessels built there, he maintains its honour and explains its decay, while he makes various suggestions for the restoration of prosperity, even to the hint that Ipswich would be a healthy and pleasant place for persons to retire to who would live well upon slender means. He writes, indeed, of Ipswich like a loyal townsman who had lived there all his life.

At Bury St. Edmunds Defoe tolls us how in a pathway between two churches a barrister of good family attempted to assassinate his brother-in-law whom he had invited with his wife and children to supper. On excuse of visiting a neighbour he led him to the ambush of a hired assassin. They left their victim for dead, horribly mangled on the head and face and body with a hedgebill. He lived to bring them to justice, and was living still when Defoe wrote. But the assassins had been condemned to death "on the statute for defacing and dismembering, called the Coventry Act." This Tour also recalls the days when Bury was a place of fashionable holiday resort. Defoe meditates upon the decline and fall of Dunwich, tells of the coming and going of the swallows from our east coast, and of innumerable swallows whom he saw one day waiting for a favourable wind on the roofs of the church and houses at Southwold. We read of the coming up to London of the Norfolk turkeys on foot, in droves of from three hundred to a thousand, and so many droves that by one route alone, and that not the most crowded—over Stratford Bridge—a hundred and forty thousand birds travelled to London between August and October.

In Norwich, Defoe was less interested than in Ipswich; but of Yarmouth his account is full, and the frequency of wrecks on the east coast, especially about Cromer Bay, which seamen called the Devil's Throat, is illustrated by the fact that in all the way from Winterton towards Cromer that "the farmers and country people had scarce a barn, or a shed, or a stable, nay not the pales of their yards and gardens, not a hog sty, but what was built of old planks, beams, wales, and timbers, etc., the wrecks of ships, and ruins of mariners' and merchants' fortunes."

Defoe saw the races at Newmarket, where he was "sick of the jockeying part." He went also to Bury Fair, of which he gives a full description, and at Cambridge he paid honour to the University.

There was another Tour told in letters so near to Defoe's in date and form that the first or second volume of one work is often sold with the second or first volume of the other. The book not by Defoe was entitled "A Journey through England in Familiar Letters from a Gentleman" here to his friend abroad, in two vols., 1722, with a third volume on Scotland in 1726. All editions published after Defoe's death in 1731 have matter added by others. The addition of new matter began with the novelist Samuel Richardson in 1732.

Some time afterwards there were changes announced as "by a gentleman of eminence in the literary world."

H. M.

TOUR THROUGH THE EASTERN COUNTIES OF ENGLAND, 1722.

I began my travels where I purpose to end them, viz., at the City of London, and therefore my account of the city itself will come last, that is to say, at the latter end of my southern progress; and as in the course of this journey I shall have many occasions to call it a circuit, if not a circle, so I chose to give it the title of circuits in the plural, because I do not pretend to have travelled it all in one journey, but in many, and some of them many times over; the better to inform myself of everything I could find worth taking notice of.

I hope it will appear that I am not the less, but the more capable of giving a full account of things, by how much the more deliberation I have taken in the view of them, and by how much the oftener I have had opportunity to see them.

I set out the 3rd of April, 1722, going first eastward, and took what I think I may very honestly call a circuit in the very letter of it; for I went down by the coast of the Thames through the Marshes or Hundreds on the south side of the county of Essex, till I came to Malden, Colchester, and Harwich, thence continuing on the coast of Suffolk to Yarmouth; thence round by the edge of the sea, on the north and west side of Norfolk, to Lynn, Wisbech, and the Wash; thence back again, on the north side of Suffolk and Essex, to the west, ending it in Middlesex, near the place where I began it, reserving the middle or centre of the several counties to some little excursions, which I made by themselves.

Passing Bow Bridge, where the county of Essex begins, the first observation I made was, that all the villages which may be called the neighbourhood of the city of London on this, as well as on the other sides thereof, which I shall speak to in their order; I say, all those villages are increased in buildings to a strange degree, within the compass of about twenty or thirty years past at the most.

The village of Stratford, the first in this county from London, is not only increased, but, I believe, more than doubled in that time; every vacancy filled up with new houses, and two little towns or hamlets, as they may be called, on the forest side of the town entirely new, namely Maryland Point and the Gravel Pits, one facing the road to Woodford and Epping, and the other facing the road to Ilford; and as for the hither part, it is almost joined to Bow, in spite of rivers, canals, marshy grounds, &c. Nor is this increase of building the case only in this and all the other villages round London; but the increase of the value and rent of the houses formerly standing has, in that compass of years above-mentioned, advanced to a very great degree, and I may venture to say at least the fifth part; some think a third part, above what they were before.

This is indeed most visible, speaking of Stratford in Essex; but it is the same thing in proportion in other villages adjacent, especially on the forest side; as at Low Leyton, Leytonstone, Walthamstow, Woodford, Wanstead, and the towns of West Ham, Plaistow, Upton, etc. In all which places, or near them (as the inhabitants say), above a thousand new foundations have been erected, besides old houses repaired, all since the Revolution; and this is not to be forgotten too, that this increase is, generally speaking, of handsome, large houses, from £20 a year to £60, very few under £20 a year; being chiefly for the habitations of the richest citizens, such as either are able to keep two houses, one in the country and one in the city; or for such citizens as being rich, and having left off trade, live altogether in these neighbouring villages, for the pleasure and health of the latter part of their days.

The truth of this may at least appear, in that they tell me there are no less than two hundred coaches kept by the inhabitants within the circumference of these few villages named above, besides such as are kept by accidental lodgers.

This increase of the inhabitants, and the cause of it, I shall enlarge upon when I come to speak of the like in the counties of Middlesex, Surrey, &c, where it is the same, only in a much greater degree. But this I must take notice of here, that this increase causes those villages to be much pleasanter and more sociable than formerly, for now people go to them, not for retirement into the country, but for good company; of which, that I may speak to the ladies as well as other authors do, there are in these villages, nay, in all, three or four excepted, excellent conversation, and a great deal of it, and that without the mixture of assemblies, gaming-houses, and public foundations of vice and debauchery; and particularly I find none of those incentives kept up on this side the country.

Mr. Camden, and his learned continuator, Bishop Gibson, have ransacked this country for its antiquities, and have left little unsearched; and as it is not my present design to say much of what has been said already, I shall touch very lightly where two such excellent antiquaries have gone before me; except it be to add what may have been since discovered, which as to these parts is only this: That there seems to be lately found out in the bottom of the Marshes (generally called Hackney Marsh, and beginning near about the place now called the Wick, between Old Ford and the said Wick), the remains of a great stone causeway, which, as it is supposed, was the highway, or great road from London into Essex, and the same which goes now over the great bridge between Bow and Stratford.

That the great road lay this way, and that the great causeway landed again just over the river, where now the Temple Mills stand, and passed by Sir Thomas Hickes's house at Ruckolls, all this is not doubted; and that it was one of those famous highways made by the Romans there is undoubted proof, by the several marks of Roman work, and by Roman coins and other antiquities found there, some of which are said to be deposited in the hands of the Rev. Mr. Strype, vicar of the parish of Low Leyton.

From hence the great road passed up to Leytonstone, a place by some known now as much by the sign of the "Green Man," formerly a lodge upon the edge of the forest; and crossing by Wanstead House, formerly the dwelling of Sir Josiah Child, now of his son the Lord Castlemain (of which hereafter), went over the same river which we now pass at Ilford; and passing that part of the great forest which we now call Hainault Forest, came into that which is now the great road, a little on this side the Whalebone, a place on the road so called because the rib-bone of a great whale, which was taken in the River Thames the same year that Oliver Cromwell died, 1658, was fixed there for a monument of that monstrous creature, it being at first about eight-and-twenty feet long.

According to my first intention of effectually viewing the sea-coast of these three counties, I went from Stratford to Barking, a large market-town, but chiefly inhabited by fishermen, whose smacks ride in the Thames, at the mouth of their river, from whence their fish is sent up to London to the market at Billingsgate by small boats, of which I shall speak by itself in my description of London.

One thing I cannot omit in the mention of these Barking fisher-smacks, viz., that one of those fishermen, a very substantial and experienced man, convinced me that all the pretences to bringing fish alive to London market from the North Seas, and other remote places on the coast of Great Britain, by the new-built sloops called fish-pools, have not been able to do anything but what their fishing-smacks are able on the same occasion to perform. These fishing-smacks are very useful vessels to the public upon many occasions; as particularly, in time of war they are used as press-smacks, running to all the northern and western coasts to pick up seamen to man the navy, when any expedition is at hand that requires a sudden equipment; at other times, being excellent sailors, they are tenders to particular men of war; and on an expedition they have been made use of as machines for the blowing up of fortified ports and havens; as at Calais, St. Malo, and other places.

This parish of Barking is very large, and by the improvement of lands taken in out of the Thames, and out of the river which runs by the town, the tithes, as the townsmen assured me, are worth above £600 per annum, including, small tithes. Note.—This parish has two or three chapels of ease, viz., one at Ilford, and one on the side of Hainault Forest, called New Chapel.

Sir Thomas Fanshaw, of an ancient Roman Catholic family, has a very good estate in this parish. A little beyond the town, on the road to Dagenham, stood a great house, ancient, and now almost fallen down, where tradition says the Gunpowder Treason Plot was at first contrived, and that all the first consultations about it were held there.

This side of the county is rather rich in land than in inhabitants, occasioned chiefly by the unhealthiness of the air; for these low marsh grounds, which, with all the south side of the county, have been saved out of the River Thames, and out of the sea, where the river is wide enough to be called so, begin here, or rather begin at West Ham, by Stratford, and continue to extend themselves, from hence eastward, growing wider and wider till we come beyond Tilbury, when the flat country lies six, seven, or eight miles broad, and is justly said to be both unhealthy and unpleasant.

However, the lands are rich, and, as is observable, it is very good farming in the marshes, because the landlords let good pennyworths, for it being a place where everybody cannot live, those that venture it will have encouragement and indeed it is but reasonable they should.

Several little observations I made in this part of the county of Essex.

1. We saw, passing from Barking to Dagenham, the famous breach, made by an inundation of the Thames, which was so great as that it laid near 5,000 acres of land under water, but which after near ten years lying under water, and being several times blown up, has been at last effectually stopped by the application of Captain Perry, the gentleman who, for several years, had been employed in the Czar of

Muscovy's works, at Veronitza, on the River Don. This breach appeared now effectually made up, and they assured us that the new work, where the breach was, is by much esteemed the strongest of all the sea walls in that level.

2. It was observable that great part of the lands in these levels, especially those on this side East Tilbury, are held by the farmers, cow-keepers, and grazing butchers who live in and near London, and that they are generally stocked (all the winter half year) with large fat sheep, viz., Lincolnshire and Leicestershire wethers, which they buy in Smithfield in September and October, when the Lincolnshire and Leicestershire graziers sell off their stock, and are kept here till Christmas, or Candlemas, or thereabouts; and though they are not made at all fatter here than they were when bought in, yet the farmer or butcher finds very good advantage in it, by the difference of the price of mutton between Michaelmas, when it is cheapest, and Candlemas, when it is dearest; this is what the butchers value themselves upon, when they tell us at the market that it is right marsh-mutton.

3. In the bottom of these Marshes, and close to the edge of the river, stands the strong fortress of Tilbury, called Tilbury Fort, which may justly be looked upon as the key of the River Thames, and consequently the key of the City of London. It is a regular fortification. The design of it was a pentagon, but the water bastion, as it would have been called, was never built. The plan was laid out by Sir Martin Beckman, chief engineer to King Charles II., who also designed the works at Sheerness. The esplanade of the fort is very large, and the bastions the largest of any in England, the foundation is laid so deep, and piles under that, driven down two an end of one another, so far, till they were assured they were below the channel of the river, and that the piles, which were shed with iron, entered into the solid chalk rock adjoining to, or reaching from, the chalk hills on the other side. These bastions settled considerably at first, as did also part of the curtain, the great quantity of earth that was brought to fill them up, necessarily, requiring to be made solid by time; but they are now firm as the rocks of chalk which they came from, and the filling up one of these bastions, as I have been told by good hands, cost the Government £6,000, being filled with chalk rubbish fetched from the chalk pits at Northfleet, just above Gravesend.

The work to the land side is complete; the bastions are faced with brick. There is a double ditch, or moat, the innermost part of which is 180 feet broad; there is a good counterscarp, and a covered way marked out with ravelins and tenailles, but they are not raised a second time after their first settling.

On the land side there are also two small redoubts of brick, but of very little strength, for the chief strength of this fort on the land side consists in this, that they are able to lay the whole level under water, and so to make it impossible for an enemy to make any approaches to the fort that way.

On the side next the river there is a very strong curtain, with a noble gate called the Water Gate in the middle, and the ditch is palisadoed. At the place where the water bastion was designed to be built, and which by the plan should run wholly out into the river, so to flank the two curtains of each side; I say, in the place where it should have been, stands a high tower, which they tell us was built in Queen Elizabeth's time, and was called the Block House; the side next the water is vacant.

Before this curtain, above and below the said vacancy, is a platform in the place of a counterscarp, on which are planted 106 pieces of cannon, generally all of them carrying from twenty-four to forty-six pound ball; a battery so terrible as well imports the consequence of that place; besides which, there are smaller pieces planted between, and the bastions and curtain also are planted with guns; so that they must be bold fellows who will venture in the biggest ships the world has heard of to pass such a battery, if the men appointed to serve the guns do their duty like stout fellows, as becomes them.

The present government of this important place is under the prudent administration of the Right Honourable the Lord Newbrugh.

From hence there is nothing for many miles together remarkable but a continued level of unhealthy marshes, called the Three Hundreds, till we come before Leigh, and to the mouth of the River Chelmer, and Blackwater. These rivers united make a large firth, or inlet of the sea, which by Mr. Camden is called Idumanum Fluvium; but by our fishermen and seamen, who use it as a port, it is called Malden Water.

In this inlet of the sea is Osey, or Osyth Island, commonly called Oosy Island, so well known by our London men of pleasure for the infinite number of wild fowl, that is to say, duck, mallard, teal, and widgeon, of which there are such vast flights, that they tell us the island, namely the creek, seems covered with them at certain times of the year, and they go from London on purpose for the pleasure of shooting; and, indeed, often come home very well laden with game. But it must be remembered too that those gentlemen who are such lovers of the sport, and go so far for it, often return with an Essex ague on their backs, which they find a heavier load than the fowls they have shot.

It is on this shore, and near this creek, that the greatest quantity of fresh fish is caught which supplies not this country only, but London markets also. On the shore, beginning a little below Candy Island, or rather below Leigh Road, there lies a great shoal or sand called the Black Tail, which runs out near three leagues into the sea due east; at the end of it stands a pole or mast, set up by the Trinity House men of London, whose business is to lay buoys and set up sea marks for the direction of the sailors; this is called Shoe Beacon, from the point of land where this sand begins, which is called Shoeburyness, and that from the town of Shoebury, which stands by it. From this sand, and on the edge of Shoebury, before it, or south west of it, all along, to the mouth of Colchester water, the shore is full of shoals and sands, with some deep channels between; all which are so full of fish, that not only the Barking fishing-smacks come hither to fish, but the whole shore is full of small fisher-boats in very great numbers, belonging to the villages and towns on the coast, who come in every tide with what they take; and selling the smaller fish in the country, send the best and largest away upon horses, which go night and day to London market.

N.B.—I am the more particular in my remarks on this place, because in the course of my travels the reader will meet with the like in almost every place of note through the whole island, where it will be seen how this whole kingdom, as well the people as the land, and even the sea, in every part of it, are employed to furnish something, and I may add, the best of everything, to supply the City of London with provisions; I mean by provisions, corn, flesh, fish, butter, cheese, salt, fuel, timber, etc., and clothes also; with everything necessary for building, and furniture for their own use or for trade; of all which in their order.

On this shore also are taken the best and nicest, though not the largest, oysters in England; the spot from whence they have their common appellation is a little bank called Woelfleet, scarce to be called an island, in the mouth of the River Crouch, now called Crooksea Water; but the chief place where the said oysters are now had is from Wyvenhoe and the shores adjacent, whither they are brought by the fishermen, who take them at the mouth of that they call Colchester water and about the sand they call the Spits, and carry them up to Wyvenhoe, where they are laid in beds or pits on the shore to feed, as they call it; and then being barrelled up and carried to Colchester, which is but three miles off, they are sent to London by land, and are from thence called Colchester oysters.

The chief sort of other fish which they carry from this part of the shore to London are soles, which they take sometimes exceeding large, and yield a very good price at London market. Also sometimes middling turbot, with whiting, codling and large flounders; the small fish, as above, they sell in the country.

In the several creeks and openings, as above, on this shore there are also other islands, but of no particular note, except Mersey, which lies in the middle of the two openings between Malden Water and Colchester Water; being of the most difficult access, so that it is thought a thousand men well provided might keep possession of it against a great force, whether by land or sea. On this account, and because if possessed by an enemy it would shut up all the navigation and fishery on that side, the Government formerly built a fort on the south-east point of it; and generally in case of Dutch war, there is a strong body of troops kept there to defend it.

At this place may be said to end what we call the Hundreds of Essex—that is to say, the three Hundreds or divisions which include the marshy country, viz., Barnstable Hundred, Rochford Hundred, and Dengy Hundred.

I have one remark more before I leave this damp part of the world, and which I cannot omit on the women's account, namely, that I took notice of a strange decay of the sex here; insomuch that all along this country it was very frequent to meet with men that had had from five or six to fourteen or fifteen wives; nay, and some more. And I was informed that in the marshes on the other side of the river over against Candy Island there was a farmer who was then living with the five-and-twentieth wife, and that his son, who was but about thirty-five years old, had already had about fourteen. Indeed, this part of the story I only had by report, though from good hands too; but the other is well known and easy to be inquired into about Fobbing, Curringham, Thundersly, Benfleet, Prittlewell, Wakering, Great Stambridge, Cricksea, Burnham, Dengy, and other towns of the like situation. The reason, as a merry fellow told me, who said he had had about a dozen and a half of wives (though I found afterwards he fibbed a little) was this: That they being bred in the marshes themselves and seasoned to the place, did pretty well with it; but that they always went up into the hilly country, or, to speak their own language, into the uplands for a wife. That when they took the young lasses out of the wholesome and fresh air they were healthy, fresh, and clear, and well; but when they came out of their native air into the marshes among the fogs and damps, there they presently changed their complexion, got an ague or two, and seldom held it above half a year, or a year at most; "And then," said he, "we go to the uplands again and fetch another;" so that marrying of wives was reckoned a kind of good farm to them. It is true the fellow told this in a kind of drollery and mirth; but the fact, for all that, is certainly true; and that they have abundance of wives by that very means. Nor is it less true that the inhabitants in these places do not hold it out, as in other countries, and as first you seldom meet with very ancient people among the poor, as in other places we do, so, take it one with another, not one-half of the inhabitants are natives of the place; but such as from other countries or in other parts of this country settle here for the advantage of good farms; for which I appeal to any impartial inquiry, having myself examined into it critically in several places.

From the marshes and low grounds being not able to travel without many windings and indentures by reason of the creeks and waters, I came up to the town of Malden, a noted market town situate at the conflux or joining of two principal rivers in this county, the Chelm or Chelmer, and the Blackwater, and where they enter into the sea. The channel, as I have noted, is called by the sailors Malden Water, and is navigable up to the town, where by that means is a great trade for carrying corn by water to London; the county of Essex being (especially on all that side) a great corn county.

When I have said this I think I have done Malden justice, and said all of it that there is to be said, unless I should run into the old story of its antiquity, and tell you it was a Roman colony in the time of Vespasian, and that it was called Camolodunum. How the Britons, under Queen Boadicea, in revenge for the Romans' ill-usage of her—for indeed they used her majesty ill—they stripped her naked and whipped her publicly through their streets for some affront she had given them. I say how for this she raised the Britons round the country, overpowered, and cut in pieces the Tenth Legion, killed above eighty thousand Romans, and destroyed the colony; but was afterwards overthrown in a great battle, and sixty thousand Britons slain. I say, unless I should enter into this story, I have nothing more to say of Malden, and, as for that story, it is so fully related by Mr. Camden in his history of the Romans in Britain at the beginning of his "Britannia," that I need only refer the reader to it, and go on with my journey.

Being obliged to come thus far into the uplands, as above, I made it my road to pass through Witham, a pleasant, well-situated market town, in which, and in its neighbourhood, there are as many gentlemen of good fortunes and families as I believe can be met with in so narrow a compass in any of the three counties of which I make this circuit.

In the town of Witham dwells the Lord Pasely, oldest son of the Earl of Abercorn of Ireland (a branch of the noble family of Hamilton, in Scotland). His lordship has a small, but a neat, well-built new house, and is finishing his gardens in such a manner as few in that part of England will exceed them.

Nearer Chelmsford, hard by Boreham, lives the Lord Viscount Barrington, who, though not born to the title, or estate, or name which he now possesses, had the honour to be twice made heir to the estates of gentlemen not at all related to him, at least, one of them, as is very much to his honour, mentioned in his patent of creation. His name was Shute, his father a linendraper in London, and served sheriff of the said city in very troublesome times. He changed the name of Shute for that of Barrington by an Act of Parliament obtained for that purpose, and had the dignity of a baron of the kingdom conferred on him by the favour of King George. His lordship is a Dissenter, and seems to love retirement. He was a member of Parliament for the town of Berwick-upon-Tweed.

On the other side of Witham, at Fauburn, an ancient mansion house, built by the Romans, lives Mr. Bullock, whose father married the daughter of that eminent citizen, Sir Josiah Child, of Wanstead, by whom she had three sons; the eldest enjoys the estate, which is considerable.

It is observable, that in this part of the country there are several very considerable estates, purchased and now enjoyed by citizens of London, merchants, and tradesmen, as Mr. Western, an iron merchant, near Kelendon; Mr. Cresnor, a wholesale grocer, who was, a little before he died, named for sheriff at Earl's Coln; Mr. Olemus, a merchant at Braintree; Mr. Westcomb, near Malden; Sir Thomas Webster at Copthall, near Waltham; and several others.

I mention this to observe how the present increase of wealth in the City of London spreads itself into the country, and plants families and fortunes, who in another age will equal the families of the ancient gentry, who perhaps were brought out. I shall take notice of this in a general head, and when I have run through all the counties, collect a list of the families of citizens and tradesmen thus established in the several counties, especially round London.

The product of all this part of the country is corn, as that of the marshy feeding grounds mentioned above is grass, where their chief business is breeding of calves, which I need not say are the best and fattest, and the largest veal in England, if not in the world; and, as an instance, I ate part of a veal or calf, fed by the late Sir Josiah Child at Wanstead, the loin of which weighed above thirty pounds, and the flesh exceeding white and fat.

From hence I went on to Colchester. The story of Kill-Dane, which is told of the town of Kelvedon, three miles from Witham, namely, that this is the place where the massacre of the Danes was begun by the women, and that therefore it was called Kill-Dane; I say of it, as we generally say of improbable news, it wants confirmation. The true name of the town is Kelvedon, and has been so for many hundred years. Neither does Mr. Camden, or any other writer I meet with worth naming, insist on this piece of empty tradition. The town is commonly called Keldon.

Colchester is an ancient corporation. The town is large, very populous, the streets fair and beautiful, and though it may not said to be finely built, yet there are abundance of very good and well-built houses in it. It still mourns in the ruins of a civil war; during which, or rather after the heat of the war was over, it suffered a severe siege, which, the garrison making a resolute defence, was turned into a blockade, in which the garrison and inhabitants also suffered the utmost extremity of hunger, and were at last obliged to surrender at discretion, when their two chief officers, Sir Charles Lucas and Sir George Lisle, were shot to death under the castle wall. The inhabitants had a tradition that no grass would grow upon the spot where the blood of those two gallant gentlemen was spilt, and they showed the place bare of grass for many years; but whether for this reason I will not affirm. The story is now dropped, and the grass, I suppose, grows there, as in other places.

However, the battered walls, the breaches in the turrets, and the ruined churches, still remain, except that the church of St. Mary (where they had the royal fort) is rebuilt; but the steeple, which was two-thirds battered down, because the besieged had a large culverin upon it that did much execution, remains still in that condition.

There is another church which bears the marks of those times, namely, on the south side of the town, in the way to the Hythe, of which more hereafter.

The lines of contravallation, with the forts built by the besiegers, and which surrounded the whole town, remain very visible in many places; but the chief of them are demolished.

The River Colne, which passes through this town, compasses it on the north and east sides, and served in those times for a complete defence on those sides. They have three bridges over it, one called North Bridge, at the north gate, by which the road leads into Suffolk; one called East Bridge, at the foot of the High Street, over which lies the road to Harwich, and one at the Hythe, as above.

The river is navigable within three miles of the town for ships of large burthen; a little lower it may receive even a royal navy; and up to that part called the Hythe, close to the houses, it is navigable for hoys and small barques. This Hythe is a long street, passing from west to east, on the south side of the town. At the west end of it, there is a small intermission of the buildings, but not much; and towards the river it is very populous (it may be called the Wapping of Colchester). There is one church in that part of the town, a large quay by the river, and a good custom-house.

The town may be said chiefly to subsist by the trade of making bays, which is known over most of the trading parts of Europe by the name of Colchester Bays, though indeed all the towns round carry on the same trade—namely, Kelvedon, Witham, Coggeshall, Braintree, Bocking, &c., and the whole county, large as it is, may be said to be employed, and in part maintained, by the spinning of wool for the bay trade of Colchester and its adjacent towns. The account of the siege, A.D. 1648, with a diary of the most remarkable passages, are as follows, which I had from so good a hand as that I have no reason to question its being a true relation.

A DIARY: OR, AN ACCOUNT OF THE SIEGE AND BLOCKADE OF COLCHESTER, A.D. 1648.

On the 4th of June, we were alarmed in the town of Colchester that the Lord Goring, the Lord Capel, and a body of two thousand of the loyal party, who had been in arms in Kent, having left a great body of an army in possession of Rochester Bridge, where they resolved to fight the Lord Fairfax and the Parliament army, had given the said General Fairfax the slip, and having passed the Thames at Greenwich, were come to Stratford, and were advancing this way; upon which news, Sir Charles Lucas, Sir George Lisle, Colonel Cook, and several gentlemen of the loyal army, and all that had commissions from the king, with a gallant appearance of gentlemen volunteers, drew together from all parts of the country to join with them.

The 8th, we were further informed that they were advanced to Chelmsford, to New Hall House, and to Witham; and the 9th some of the horse arrived in the town, taking possession of the gates, and having engineers with them, told us that General Goring had resolved to make this town his headquarters, and would cause it to be well fortified. They also caused the drums to beat for volunteers; and a good number of the poor bay-weavers, and such-like people, wanting employment, enlisted; so that they completed Sir Charles Lucas's regiment, which was but thin, to near eight hundred men.

On the 10th we had news that the Lord Fairfax, having beaten the Royalists at Maidstone, and retaken Rochester, had passed the Thames at Gravesend, though with great difficulty, and with some loss, and was come to Horndon-on-the-Hill, in order to gain Colchester before the Royalists; but that hearing Sir Charles Lucas had prevented him, had ordered his rendezvous at Billerecay, and intended to possess the pass at Malden on the 11th, where Sir Thomas Honnywood, with the county-trained bands, was to be the same day.

The same evening the Lord Goring, with all his forces, making about five thousand six hundred men, horse and foot, came to Colchester, and encamping without the suburbs, under command of the cannon of St. Mary's fort, made disposition to fight the Parliament forces if they came up.

The 12th, the Lord Goring came into Colchester, viewed the fort in St. Mary's churchyard, ordered more cannon to be planted upon it, posted two regiments in the suburbs without the head gate, let the town know he would take them into his Majesty's protection, and that he would fight the enemy in that situation. The same evening the Lord Fairfax, with a strong party of one thousand horse, came to Lexden, at two small miles' distance, expecting the rest of his army there the same night.

The Lord Goring brought in prisoners the same day, Sir William Masham, and several other gentlemen of the county, who were secured under a strong guard; which the Parliament hearing, ordered twenty prisoners of the royal party to be singled out, declaring, that they should be used in the same manner as the Lord Goring used Sir William Masham, and the gentlemen prisoners with him.

On the 13th, early in the morning, our spies brought intelligence that the Lord Fairfax, all his forces being come up to him, was making dispositions for a march, resolving to attack the Royalists in their camp; upon which, the Lord Goring drew all his forces together, resolving to fight. The engineers had offered the night before to entrench his camp, and to draw a line round it in one night's time, but his lordship declined it, and now there was no time for it; whereupon the general, Lord Goring, drew up his army in order of battle on both sides the road, the horse in the open fields on the wings; the foot were drawn up, one regiment in the road, one regiment on each side, and two regiments for reserve in the suburb, just at the entrance of the town, with a regiment of volunteers advanced as a forlorn hope, and a regiment of horse at the head-gate, ready to support the reserve, as occasion should require.

About nine in the morning we heard the enemy's drums beat a march, and in half an hour more their first troops appeared on the higher grounds towards Lexden. Immediately the cannon from St. Mary's fired upon them, and put some troops of horse into confusion, doing great execution, which, they not being able to shun it, made them quicken their pace, fall on, when our cannon were obliged to cease firing, lest we should hurt our own troops as well as the enemy. Soon after, their foot appeared, and our cannon saluted them in like manner, and killed them a great many men.

Their first line of foot was led up by Colonel Barkstead, and consisted of three regiments of foot, making about 1,700 men, and these charged our regiment in the lane, commanded by Sir George Lisle and Sir William Campion. They fell on with great fury, and were received with as much gallantry, and three times repulsed; nor could they break in here, though the Lord Fairfax sent fresh men to support them, till the Royalists' horse, oppressed with numbers on the left, were obliged to retire, and at last to come full gallop into the street, and so on into the town. Nay, still the foot stood firm, and the volunteers, being all gentlemen, kept their ground with the greatest resolution; but the left wing being routed, as above, Sir William Campion was obliged to make a front to the left, and lining the hedge with his musketeers, made a stand with a body of pikes against the enemy's horse, and prevented them entering the lane. Here that gallant gentleman was killed with a carabine shot; and after a very gallant resistance, the horse on the right being also overpowered, the word was given to retreat, which, however, was done in such good order, the regiments of reserve standing drawn up at the end of the street, ready to receive the enemy's horse upon the points of their pikes, that the royal troops came on in the openings between the regiments, and entered the town with very little loss, and in very good order.

By this, however, those regiments of reserve were brought at last to sustain the efforts of the enemy's whole army, till being overpowered by numbers they were put into disorder, and forced to get into the town in the best manner they could; by which means near two hundred men were killed or made prisoners.

Encouraged by this success the enemy pushed on, supposing they should enter the town pell-mell with the rest; nor did the Royalists hinder them, but let good part of Barkstead's own regiment enter the head-gate; but then sallying from St. Mary's with a choice body of foot on their left, and the horse rallying in the High Street, and charging them again in the front, they were driven back quite into the street of the suburb, and most of those that had so rashly entered were cut in pieces.

Thus they were repulsed at the south entrance into the town; and though they attempted to storm three times after that with great resolution, yet they were as often beaten back, and that with great havoc of their men; and the cannon from the fort all the while did execution upon those who stood drawn up to support them; so that at last, seeing no good to be done, they retreated, having small joy of their pretended victory.

They lost in this action Colonel Needham, who commanded a regiment called the Tower Guards, and who fought very desperately; Captain Cox, an old experienced horse officer, and several other officers of note, with a great many private men, though, as they had the field, they concealed their number, giving out that they lost but a hundred, when we were assured they lost near a thousand men besides the wounded.

They took some of our men prisoners, occasioned by the regiment of Colonel Farr, and two more sustaining the shock of their whole army, to secure the retreat of the main body, as above.

The 14th, the Lord Fairfax finding he was not able to carry the town by storm, without the formality of a siege, took his headquarters at Lexden, and sent to London and to Suffolk for more forces; also he ordered the trained bands to be raised and posted on the roads to prevent succours. Notwithstanding which, divers gentlemen, with some assistance of men and arms, found means to get into the town.

The very same night they began to break ground, and particularly to raise a fort between Colchester and Lexden, to cover the general's quarter from the sallies from the town; for the Royalists having a good body of horse, gave them no rest, but scoured the fields every day, and falling all that were found straggling from their posts, and by this means killed a great many.

The 17th, Sir Charles Lucas having been out with 1,200 horse, and detaching parties toward the seaside, and towards Harwich, they brought in a very great quantity of provisions, and abundance of sheep and black cattle sufficient for the supply of the town for a considerable time; and had not the Suffolk forces advanced over Cataway Bridge to prevent it, a larger supply had been brought in that way; for now it appeared plainly that the Lord Fairfax finding the garrison strong and resolute, and that he was not in a condition to reduce them by force, at least without the loss of much blood, had resolved to turn his siege into a blockade, and reduce them by hunger; their troops being also wanted to oppose several other parties, who had, in several parts of the kingdom, taken arms for the king's cause.

This same day General Fairfax sent in a trumpet to propose exchanging prisoners, which the Lord Goring rejected, expecting a reinforcement of troops, which were actually coming to him, and were to be at Linton in Cambridgeshire as the next day.

The same day two ships brought in a quantity of corn and provisions and fifty-six men from the shore of Kent with several gentlemen, who all landed and came up to the town, and the greatest part of the corn was with the utmost application unloaded the same night into some hoys, which brought it up to the Hythe, being apprehensive of the Parliament's ships which lay at Harwich, who having intelligence of the said ships, came the next day into the mouth of the river, and took the said two ships and what corn was left in them. The besieged sent out a party to help the ships, but having no boats they could not assist them.

18th. Sir Charles Lucas sent an answer about exchange of prisoners, accepting the conditions offered, but the Parliament's general returned that he would not treat with Sir Charles, for that he (Sir Charles) being his prisoner upon his parole of honour, and having appeared in arms contrary to the rules of war, had forfeited his honour and faith, and was not capable of command or trust in martial affairs. To this

Sir Charles sent back an answer, and his excuse for his breach of his parole, but it was not accepted, nor would the Lord Fairfax enter upon any treaty with him.

Upon this second message Sir William Masham and the Parliament Committee and other gentlemen, who were prisoners in the town, sent a message in writing under their hands to the Lord Fairfax, entreating him to enter into a treaty for peace; but the Lord Fairfax returned, he could take no notice of their request, as supposing it forced from them under restraint; but that if the Lord Goring desired peace, he might write to the Parliament, and he would cause his messenger to have a safe conduct to carry his letter. There was a paper sent enclosed in this paper, signed Capel, Norwich, Charles Lucas, but to that the general would return no answer, because it was signed by Sir Charles for the reasons above.

All this while the Lord Goring, finding the enemy strengthening themselves, gave order for fortifying the town, and drawing lines in several places to secure the entrance, as particularly without the east bridge, and without the north gate and bridge, and to plant more cannon upon the works; to which end some great guns were brought in from some ships at Wivenhoe.

The same day, our men sallied out in three places, and attacked the besiegers, first at their port, called Essex, then at their new works, on the south of the town; a third party sallying at the east bridge, brought in some booty from the Suffolk troops, having killed several of their stragglers on the Harwich road. They also took a lieutenant of horse prisoner, and brought him into the town.

19th. This day we had the unwelcome news that our friends at Linton were defeated by the enemy, and Major Muschamp, a loyal gentleman, killed.

The same night, our men gave the enemy alarm at their new Essex fort, and thereby drew them out as if they would fight, till they brought them within reach of the cannon of St. Mary's, and then our men retiring, the great guns let fly among them, and made them run. Our men shouted after them. Several of them were killed on this occasion, one shot having killed three horsemen in our fight.

20th. We now found the enemy, in order to a perfect blockade, resolved to draw a line of circumvallation round the town; having received a train of forty pieces of heavy cannon from the Tower of London.

This day the Parliament sent a messenger to their prisoners to know how they fared, and how they were used; who returned word, that they fared indifferent well, and were very civilly used, but that provisions were scarce, and therefore dear.

This day a party of horse, with 300 foot, sallied out, and marched as far as the fort on the Isle of Mersey, which they made a show of attacking, to keep in the garrison. Meanwhile the rest took a good number of cattle from the country, which they brought safe into the town, with five waggons laden with corn. This was the last they could bring in that way, the lines being soon finished on that side.

This day the Lord Fairfax sent in a trumpet to the Earl of Norwich and the Lord Goring, offering honourable conditions to them all, allowing all the gentlemen their lives and arms, exemption from plunder, and passes, if they desired to go beyond sea, and all the private men pardon, and leave to go peaceably to their own dwellings. But the Lord Goring and the rest of the gentlemen rejected it, and laughed at them, upon which the Lord Fairfax made proclamation, that his men should give the private soldiers in Colchester free leave to pass through their camp, and go where they pleased without molestation, only leaving their arms, but that the gentlemen should have no quarter. This was a great loss to the Royalists, for now the men foreseeing the great hardships they were like to suffer, began to slip away, and the Lord Goring was obliged to forbid any to desert on pain of present death, and to keep parties of horse continually patrolling to prevent them; notwithstanding which many got away.

21st. The town desired the Lord Goring to give them leave to send a message to Lord Fairfax, to desire they might have liberty to carry on their trade and sell their bays and says, which Lord Goring granted; but the enemy's general returned, that they should have considered that before they let the Royalists into the town; that to desire a free trade from a town besieged was never heard of, or at least, was such a motion, as was never yet granted; that, however, he would give the bay-makers leave to bring their bays and says, and other goods, once a week, or oftener, if they desire it, to Lexden Heath, where they should have a free market, and might sell them or carry them back again, if not sold, as they found occasion.

22nd. The besieged sallied out in the night with a strong party, and disturbed the enemy in their works, and partly ruined one of their forts, called Ewer's Fort, where the besiegers were laying a bridge over the River Colne. Also they sallied again at east bridge, and faced the Suffolk troops, who were now declared enemies. These brought in six-and-fifty good bullocks, and some cows, and they took and killed several of the enemy.

23rd. The besiegers began to fire with their cannon from Essex Fort, and from Barkstead's Fort, which was built upon the Malden road; and finding that the besieged had a party in Sir Harbottle Grimston's house, called, "The Fryery," they fired at it with their cannon, and battered it almost down, and then the soldiers set it on fire.

This day upon the townsmen's treaty for the freedom of the bay trade, the Lord Fairfax sent a second offer of conditions to the besieged, being the same as before, only excepting Lord Goring, Lord Capel, Sir George Lisle, and Sir Charles Lucas.

This day we had news in the town that the Suffolk forces were advanced to assist the besiegers, and that they began a fort called Fort Suffolk, on the north side of the town, to shut up the Suffolk road towards Stratford. This day the besieged sallied out at north bridge, attacked the out-guards of the Suffolk men on Mile End Heath, and drove them into their fort in the woods.

This day the Lord Fairfax sent a trumpet, complaining of chewed and poisoned bullets being shot from the town, and threatening to give no quarter if that practice was allowed; but Lord Goring returned answer, with a protestation, that no such thing was done by his order or consent.

24th. They fired hard from their cannon against St. Mary's steeple, on which was planted a large culverin, which annoyed them even in the general's headquarters at Lexden. One of the best gunners the garrison had was killed with a cannon bullet. This night the besieged sallied towards Audly, on the Suffolk road, and brought in some cattle.

25th. Lord Capel sent a trumpet to the Parliament-General, but the rogue ran away, and came not back, nor sent any answer; whether they received his message or not, was not known.

26th. This day having finished their new bridge, a party of their troops passed that bridge, and took post on the hill over against Mile End Church, where they built a fort, called Fothergall's Fort, and another on the east side of the road, called Rainsbro's Fort, so that the town was entirely shut in, on that side, and the Royalists had no place free but over east bridge, which was afterwards cut off by the enemy's bringing their line from the Hythe within the river to the stone causeway leading to the east bridge.

July 1st. From the 26th to the 1st, the besiegers continued finishing their works, and by the 2nd the whole town was shut in; at which the besiegers gave a general salvo from their cannon at all their forts; but the besieged gave them a return, for they sallied out in the night, attacked Barkstead's fort, scarce finished, with such fury, that they twice entered the work sword in hand, killed most part of the defendants, and spoiled part of the forts cast up; but fresh forces coming up, they retired with little loss, bringing eight prisoners, and having slain, as they reported, above 100.

On the second, Lord Fairfax offered exchange for Sir William Masham in particular, and afterwards for other prisoners, but the Lord Goring refused.

5th. The besieged sallied with two regiments, supported by some horse, at midnight; they were commanded by Sir George Lisle. They fell on with such fury, that the enemy were put into confusion, their works at east bridge ruined, and two pieces of cannon taken, Lieutenant Colonel Sambrook, and several other officers, were killed, and our men retired into the town, bringing the captain, two lieutenants, and about fifty men with them prisoners into the town; but having no horse, we could not bring off the cannon, but they spiked them, and made them unfit for service.

From this time to the 11th, the besieged sallied almost every night, being encouraged by their successes, and they constantly cut off some of the enemy, but not without loss also on their own side.

About this time we received by a spy the bad news of defeating the king's friends almost in all parts of England, and particularly several parties which had good wishes to our gentlemen, and intended to relieve them.

Our batteries from St. Mary's Fort and steeple, and from the north bridge, greatly annoyed them, and killed most of their gunners and firemen. One of the messengers who brought news to Lord Fairfax of the defeat of one of the parties, in Kent, and the taking of Weymer Castle, slipped into the town, and brought a letter to the Lord Goring, and listed in the regiment of the Lord Capel's horse.

14th. The besiegers attacked and took the Hythe Church, with a small work the besieged had there, but the defenders retired in time; some were taken prisoners in the church, but not in the fort; Sir Charles Lucas's horse was attacked by a great body of the besiegers; the besieged defended themselves with good resolution for some time, but a hand-grenade thrown in by the assailants, having fired the magazine, the house was blown up, and most of the gallant defenders buried in the ruins. This was a great blow to the Royalists, for it was a very strong pass, and always well guarded.

15th. The Lord Fairfax sent offers of honourable conditions to the soldiers of the garrison if they would surrender, or quit the service; upon which the Lords Goring and Capel, and Sir Charles Lucas, returned an answer signed by their hands, that it was not honourable or agreeable to the usage of war to offer conditions separately to the soldiers, exclusive of their officers, and therefore civilly desired his lordship to send no more such messages or proposals, or if he did, that he would not take it ill if they hanged up the messenger.

This evening all the gentlemen volunteers, with all the horse of the garrison, with Sir Charles Lucas, Sir George Lisle, and Sir Bernard Gascoigne at the head of them, resolved to break through the enemy, and forcing a pass to advance into Suffolk by Nayland Bridge. To this purpose they passed the river near Middle Mill; but their guides having misled them the enemy took the alarm; upon which their guides, and some pioneers which they had with them to open the hedges and level the banks, for their passing to Boxted, all ran away, so the horse were obliged to retreat, the enemy pretending to pursue, but thinking they had retreated by the north bridge, they missed them; upon which being enraged, they fired the suburbs without the bridge, and burned them quite down.

18th. Some of the horse attempted to escape the same way, and had the whole body been there as before, they had effected it; but there being but two troops, they were obliged to retire. Now the town began to be greatly distressed, provisions failing, and the townspeople, which were numerous, being very uneasy, and no way of breaking through being found practicable, the gentlemen would have joined in any attempt wherein they might die gallantly with their swords in their hands, but nothing presented; they often sallied and cut off many of the enemy, but their numbers were continually supplied, and the besieged diminished; their horse also sunk and became unfit for service, having very little hay, and no corn, and at length they were forced to kill them for food; so that they began to be in a very miserable condition, and the soldiers deserted every day in great numbers, not being able to bear the want of food, as being almost starved with hunger.

22nd. The Lord Fairfax offered again an exchange of prisoners, but the Lord Goring rejected it, because they refused conditions to the chief gentlemen of the garrison.

During this time, two troops of the Royal Horse sallied out in the night, resolving to break out or die: the first rode up full gallop to the enemy's horse guards on the side of Malden road, and exchanged their pistols with the advanced troops, and wheeling made as if they would retire to the town; but finding they were not immediately pursued, they wheeled about to the right, and passing another guard at a distance, without being perfectly discovered, they went clean off, and passing towards Tiptree Heath, and having good guides, they made their escape towards Cambridgeshire, in which length of way they found means to disperse without being attacked, and went every man his own way as fate directed; nor did we hear that many of them were taken: they were led, as we are informed, by Sir Bernard Gascoigne.

Upon these attempts of the horse to break out, the enemy built a small fort in the meadow right against the ford in the river at the Middle Mill, and once set that mill on fire, but it was extinguished without much damage; however, the fort prevented any more attempts that way.

22nd. The Parliament-General sent in a trumpet, to propose again the exchange of prisoners, offering the Lord Capel's son for one, and Mr. Ashburnham for Sir William Masham; but the Lord Capel, Lord Goring, and the rest of the loyal gentlemen rejected it; and Lord Capel, in particular, sent the Lord Fairfax word it was inhuman to surprise his son, who was not in arms, and offer him to insult a father's affection, but that he might murder his son if he pleased, he would leave his blood to be revenged as Heaven should give opportunity; and the Lord Goring sent word, that as they had reduced the king's servants to eat horseflesh, the prisoners should feed as they fed.

The enemy sent again to complain of the Royalists shooting poisoned bullets, and sent two affidavits of it made by two deserters, swearing it was done by the Lord Norwich's direction; the generals in the town returned under all their hands that they never gave any such command or direction; that they disowned the practice; and that the fellows who swore it were perjured before in running from their colours and the service of their king, and ought not to be credited again; but they added, that for shooting rough-cast slugs they must excuse them, as things stood with them at that time.

About this time, a porter in a soldier's habit got through the enemy's leaguer, and passing their out-guards in the dark, got into the town, and brought letters from London, assuring the Royalists that there were so many strong parties up in arms for the king, and in so many places, that they would be very suddenly relieved. This they caused to be read to the soldiers to encourage them; and particularly it related to the rising of the Earl of Holland, and the Duke of Buckingham, who with 500 horse were gotten together in arms about Kingston in Surrey; but we had notice in a few days after that they were defeated, and the Earl of Holland taken, who was afterwards beheaded.

26th. The enemy now began to batter the walls, and especially on the west side, from St. Mary's towards the north gate; and we were assured they intended a storm; on which the engineers were directed to make trenches behind the walls where the breaches should be made, that in case of a storm they might meet with a warm reception. Upon this, they gave over the design of storming. The Lord Goring finding that the enemy had set the suburbs on fire right against the Hythe, ordered the remaining houses, which were empty of inhabitants, from whence their musketeer fired against the town, to be burned also.

31st. A body of foot sallied out at midnight, to discover what the enemy were doing at a place where they thought a new fort raising; they fell in among the workmen, and put them to flight, cut in pieces several of the guard, and brought in the officer who commanded them prisoner.

August 2nd. The town was now in a miserable condition: the soldiers searched and rifled the houses of the inhabitants for victuals; they had lived on horseflesh several weeks, and most of that also was as lean as carrion, which not being well salted bred wens; and this want of diet made the soldiers sickly, and many died of fluxes, yet they boldly rejected all offers of surrender, unless with safety to their offices. However, several hundreds got out, and either passed the enemy's guards, or surrendered to them and took passes.

7th. The townspeople became very uneasy to the soldiers, and the mayor of the town, with the aldermen, waited upon the general, desiring leave to send to the Lord Fairfax for leave to all the inhabitants to come out of the town, that they might not perish, to which the Lord Goring consented, but the Lord Fairfax refused them.

12th. The rabble got together in a vast crowd about the Lord Goring's quarters, clamouring for a surrender, and they did this every evening, bringing women and children, who lay howling and crying on the ground for bread; the soldiers beat off the men, but the women and children would not stir, bidding the soldiers kill them, saying they had rather be shot than be starved.

16th. The general, moved by the cries and distress of the poor inhabitants, sent out a trumpet to the Parliament-General, demanding leave to send to the Prince, who was with a fleet of nineteen men of war in the mouth of the Thames, offering to surrender, if they were not relieved in twenty days. The Lord Fairfax refused it, and sent them word he would be in the town in person, and visit them in less than twenty days, intimating that they were preparing for a storm. Some tart messages and answers were exchanged on this occasion. The Lord Goring sent word they were willing, in compassion to the poor townspeople, and to save that effusion of blood, to surrender upon honourable terms, but that as for the storming them, which was threatened, they might come on when they thought fit, for that they (the Royalists) were ready for them. This held to the 19th.

20th. The Lord Fairfax returned what he said was his last answer, and should be the last offer of mercy. The conditions offered were, that upon a peaceable surrender, all soldiers and officers under the degree of a captain in commission should have their lives, be exempted from plunder, and have passes to go to their respective dwellings. All the captains and superior officers, with all the lords and gentlemen, as well in commission as volunteers, to surrender prisoners at discretion, only that they should not be plundered by the soldiers.

21st. The generals rejected those offers; and when the people came about them again for bread, set open one of the gates, and bid them go out to the enemy, which a great many did willingly; upon which the Lord Goring ordered all the rest that came about his door to be turned out after them. But when the people came to the Lord Fairfax's camp the out-guards were ordered to fire at them and drive them all back again to the gate, which the Lord Goring seeing, he ordered them to be received in again. And now, although the generals and soldiers also were resolute to die with their swords in their hands rather than yield, and had maturely resolved to abide a storm, yet the Mayor and Aldermen having petitioned them as well as the inhabitants, being wearied with the importunities of the distressed people, and pitying the deplorable condition they were reduced to, they agreed to enter upon a treaty, and accordingly sent out some officers to the Lord Fairfax, the Parliament-General, to treat, and with them was sent two gentlemen of the prisoners upon their parole to return.

Upon the return of the said messengers with the Lord Fairfax's terms, the Lord Goring, &c., sent out a letter declaring they would die with their swords in their hands rather than yield without quarter for life, and sent a paper of articles on which they were willing to surrender. But in the very interim of this treaty news came that the Scots army, under Duke Hamilton, which was entered into Lancashire, and was joined by the Royalists in that country, making 21,000 men, were entirely defeated. After this the Lord Fairfax would not grant any abatement of articles—viz., to have all above lieutenants surrender at mercy.

Upon this the Lord Goring and the General refused to submit again, and proposed a general sally, and to break through or die, but found upon preparing for it that the soldiers, who had their lives offered them, declined it, fearing the gentlemen would escape, and they should be left to the mercy of the Parliament soldiers; and that upon this they began to mutiny and talk of surrendering the town and their officers too. Things being brought to this pass, the Lords and General laid aside that design, and found themselves obliged to submit; and so the town was surrendered the 28th of August, 1648, upon conditions as follows:—

The Lords and gentlemen all prisoners at mercy.

The common soldiers had passes to go home to their several dwellings, but without arms, and an oath not to serve against the Parliament.

The town to be preserved from pillage, paying £14,000 ready money.

The same day a council of war being called about the prisoners of war, it was resolved that the Lords should be left to the disposal of the Parliament. That Sir Charles Lucas, Sir George Lisle, and Sir

Marmaduke Gascoigne should be shot to death, and the other officers prisoners to remain in custody till further order.

The two first of the three gentlemen were shot to death, and the third respited. Thus ended the siege of Colchester.

N.B.—Notwithstanding the number killed in the siege, and dead of the flux, and other distempers occasioned by bad diet, which were very many, and notwithstanding the number which deserted and escaped in the time of their hardships, yet there remained at the time of the surrender:

Earl of Norwich (Goring).
Lord Capell.
Lord Loughbro'.
11 Knights.
9 Colonels.
8 Lieut.-Colonels.
9 Majors.
30 Captains.
72 Lieutenants.
69 Ensigns.
183 Serjeants and Corporals.
3,067 Private Soldiers.
65 Servants to the Lords and General Officers and Gentlemen.
3,526 in all.

The town of Colchester has been supposed to contain about 40,000 people, including the out-villages which are within its liberty, of which there are a great many—the liberty of the town being of a great extent. One sad testimony of the town being so populous is that they buried upwards of 5,259 people in the plague year, 1665. But the town was severely visited indeed, even more in proportion than any of its neighbours, or than the City of London.

The government of the town is by a mayor, high steward, a recorder or his deputy, eleven aldermen, a chamberlain, a town clerk, assistants, and eighteen common councilmen. Their high steward (this year, 1722) is Sir Isaac Rebow, a gentleman of a good family and known character, who has generally for above thirty years been one of their representatives in Parliament. He has a very good house at the entrance in at the south, or head gate of the town, where he has had the honour several times to lodge and entertain the late King William of glorious memory in his returning from Holland by way of Harwich to London. Their recorder is Earl Cowper, who has been twice Lord High Chancellor of England. But his lordship not residing in those parts has put in for his deputy,—Price, Esq., barrister-at-law, and who dwells in the town. There are in Colchester eight churches besides those which are damaged, and five meeting-houses, whereof two for Quakers, besides a Dutch church and a French church.

Public Edifices are—

1. Bay Hall, an ancient society kept up for ascertaining the manufacture of bays, which are, or ought to be, all brought to this hall to be viewed and sealed according to their goodness by the masters; and to this practice has been owing the great reputation of the Colchester bays in foreign markets, where to open the side of a bale and show the seal has been enough to give the buyer a character of the value of

the goods without any further search; and so far as they abate the integrity and exactness of their method, which I am told of late is much omitted; I say, so far, that reputation will certainly abate in the markets they go to, which are principally in Portugal and Italy. This corporation is governed by a particular set of men who are called governors of the Dutch Bay Hall. And in the same building is the Dutch church.

2. The guildhall of the town, called by them the moot hall, to which is annexed the town gaol.

3. The workhouse, being lately enlarged, and to which belongs a corporation or a body of the inhabitants, consisting of sixty persons incorporated by Act of Parliament Anno 1698 for taking care of the poor. They are incorporated by the name and title of the governor, deputy governor, assistants, and guardians of the poor of the town of Colchester. They are in number eight-and-forty, to whom are added the mayor and aldermen for the time being, who are always guardians by the same charter. These make the number of sixty, as above. There is also a grammar free-school, with a good allowance to the master, who is chosen by the town.

4. The castle of Colchester is now become only a monument showing the antiquity of the place, it being built as the walls of the town also are, with Roman bricks, and the Roman coins dug up here, and ploughed up in the fields adjoining, confirm it. The inhabitants boast much that Helena, the mother of Constantine the Great, first Christian Emperor of the Romans, was born there, and it may be so for aught we know. I only observe what Mr. Camden says of the Castle of Colchester, viz.: In the middle of this city stands a castle ready to fall with age.

Though this castle has stood one hundred and twenty years from the time Mr. Camden wrote that account, and it is not fallen yet, nor will another hundred and twenty years, I believe, make it look one jot the older. And it was observable that in the late siege of this town, a common shot, which the besiegers made at this old castle, were so far from making it fall, that they made little or no impression upon it; for which reason, it seems, and because the garrison made no great use of it against the besiegers, they fired no more at it.

There are two charity schools set up here, and carried on by a generous subscription, with very good success.

The title of Colchester is in the family of Earl Rivers, and the eldest son of that family is called Lord Colchester, though as I understand, the title is not settled by the creation to the eldest son till he enjoys the title of earl with it, but that the other is by the courtesy of England; however, this I take ad referendum.

From Colchester I took another step down to the coast; the land running out a great way into the sea, south and south-east makes that promontory of land called the Naze, and well known to seamen using the northern trade. Here one sees a sea open as an ocean without any opposite shore, though it be no more than the mouth of the Thames. This point called the Naze, and the north-east point of Kent, near Margate, called the North Foreland, making what they call the mouth of the river and the port of London, though it be here above sixty miles over.

At Walton-under-the-Naze they find on the shore copperas-stone in great quantities; and there are several large works called copperas houses, where they make it with great expense.

On this promontory is a new mark erected by the Trinity House men, and at the public expense, being a round brick tower, near eighty feet high. The sea gains so much upon the land here by the continual winds at south-west, that within the memory of some of the inhabitants there they have lost above thirty acres of land in one place.

From hence we go back into the county about four miles, because of the creeks which lie between; and then turning east again come to Harwich, on the utmost eastern point of this large country.

Harwich is a town so well known and so perfectly described by many writers, I need say little of it. It is strong by situation, and may be made more so by art. But it is many years since the Government of England have had any occasion to fortify towns to the landward; it is enough that the harbour or road, which is one of the best and securest in England, is covered at the entrance by a strong fort and a battery of guns to the seaward, just as at Tilbury, and which sufficiently defend the mouth of the river. And there is a particular felicity in this fortification, viz., that though the entrance or opening of the river into the sea is very wide, especially at high-water, at least two miles, if not three over; yet the Channel, which is deep, and in which the ships must keep and come to the harbour, is narrow, and lies only on the side of the fort, so that all the ships which come in or go out must come close under the guns of the fort—that is to say, under the command of their shot.

The fort is on the Suffolk side of the bay or entrance, but stands so far into the sea upon the point of a sand or shoal, which runs out toward the Essex side, as it were, laps over the mouth of that haven like a blind to it; and our surveyors of the country affirm it to be in the county of Essex. The making this place, which was formerly no other than a sand in the sea, solid enough for the foundation of so good a fortification, has not been done but by many years' labour, often repairs, and an infinite expense of money, but it is now so firm that nothing of storms and high tides, or such things as make the sea dangerous to these kind of works, can affect it.

The harbour is of a vast extent; for, as two rivers empty themselves here, viz., Stour from Manningtree and the Orwell from Ipswich, the channels of both are large and deep; and safe for all weathers; so where they join they make a large bay or road able to receive the biggest ships, and the greatest number that ever the world saw together; I mean ships of war. In the old Dutch war great use has been made of this harbour; and I have known that there has been one hundred sail of men-of-war and their attendants and between three and four hundred sail of collier ships all in this harbour at a time, and yet none of them crowding or riding in danger of one another.

Harwich is known for being the port where the packet boats, between England and Holland, go out and come in. The inhabitants are far from being famed for good usage to strangers, but, on the contrary, are blamed for being extravagant in their reckonings in the public-houses, which has not a little encouraged the setting up of sloops, which they now call passage boats, to Holland, to go directly from the River Thames; this, though it may be something the longer passage, yet as they are said to be more obliging to passengers and more reasonable in the expense, and, as some say, also, the vessels are better sea boats, has been the reason why so many passengers do not go or come by the way of Harwich as formerly were wont to do; insomuch that the stage coaches between this place and London, which ordinarily went twice or three times a week, are now entirely laid down, and the passengers are left to hire coaches on purpose, take post-horses, or hire horses to Colchester, as they find most convenient.

The account of a petrifying quality in the earth here, though some will have it to be in the water of a spring hard by, is very strange. They boast that their town is walled and their streets paved with clay, and yet that one is as strong and the other as clean as those that are built or paved with stone. The fact is indeed true, for there is a sort of clay in the cliff, between the town and the Beacon Hill adjoining, which, when it falls down into the sea, where it is beaten with the waves and the weather, turns gradually into stone. But the chief reason assigned is from the water of a certain spring or well, which, rising in the said cliff, runs down into the sea among those pieces of clay, and petrifies them as it runs; and the force of the sea often stirring, and perhaps turning, the lumps of clay, when storms of wind may give force enough to the water, causes them to harden everywhere alike; otherwise those which were not quite sunk in the water of the spring would be petrified but in part. These stones are gathered up to pave the streets and build the houses, and are indeed very hard. It is also remarkable that some of them taken up before they are thoroughly petrified will, upon breaking them, appear to be hard as a stone without and soft as clay in the middle; whereas others that have lain a due time shall be thorough stone to the centre, and as exceeding hard within as without. The same spring is said to turn wood into iron. But this I take to be no more or less than the quality, which, as I mentioned of the shore at the Naze, is found to be in much of the stone all along this shore, viz., of the copperas kind; and it is certain that the copperas stone (so called) is found in all that cliff, and even where the water of this spring has run; and I presume that those who call the hardened pieces of wood, which they take out of this well by the name of iron, never tried the quality of it with the fire or hammer; if they had, perhaps they would have given some other account of it.

On the promontory of land which they call Beacon Hill and which lies beyond or behind the town towards the sea, there is a lighthouse to give the ships directions in their sailing by as well as their coming into the harbour in the night. I shall take notice of these again all together when I come to speak of the Society of Trinity House, as they are called, by whom they are all directed upon this coast.

This town was erected into a marquisate in honour of the truly glorious family of Schomberg, the eldest son of Duke Schomberg, who landed with King William, being styled Marquis of Harwich; but that family (in England, at least) being extinct the title dies also.

Harwich is a town of hurry and business, not much of gaiety and pleasure; yet the inhabitants seem warm in their nests, and some of them are very wealthy. There are not many (if any) gentlemen or families of note either in the town or very near it. They send two members to Parliament; the present are Sir Peter Parker and Humphrey Parsons, Esq.

And now being at the extremity of the county of Essex, of which I have given you some view as to that side next the sea only, I shall break off this part of my letter by telling you that I will take the towns which lie more towards the centre of the county, in my return by the north and west part only, that I may give you a few hints of some towns which were near me in my route this way, and of which being so well known there is but little to say.

On the road from London to Colchester, before I came into it at Witham, lie four good market towns at equal distance from one another, namely, Romford, noted for two markets, viz., one for calves and hogs, the other for corn and other provisions, most, if not all, bought up for London market. At the farther end of the town, in the middle of a stately park, stood Guldy Hall, vulgarly Giddy Hall, an ancient seat of one Coke, sometime Lord Mayor of London, but forfeited on some occasion to the Crown. It is since pulled down to the ground, and there now stands a noble stately fabric or mansion house, built upon the spot by Sir John Eyles, a wealthy merchant of London, and chosen Sub-Governor of the South Sea Company immediately after the ruin of the former Sub-Governor and Directors, whose overthrow makes the history of these times famous.

Brentwood and Ingatestone, and even Chelmsford itself, have very little to be said of them, but that they are large thoroughfare towns, full of good inns, and chiefly maintained by the excessive multitude of carriers and passengers which are constantly passing this way to London with droves of cattle, provisions, and manufactures for London.

The last of these towns is indeed the county town, where the county gaol is kept, and where the assizes are very often held; it stands on the conflux of two rivers—the Chelmer, whence the town is called, and the Cann.

At Lees, or Lee's Priory, as some call it, is to be seen an ancient house in the middle of a beautiful park, formerly the seat of the late Duke of Manchester, but since the death of the duke it is sold to the Duchess Dowager of Buckinghamshire, the present Duke of Manchester retiring to his ancient family seat at Kimbolton in Huntingdonshire, it being a much finer residence. His grace is lately married to a daughter of the Duke of Montagu by a branch of the house of Marlborough.

Four market towns fill up the rest of this part of the country—Dunmow, Braintree, Thaxted, and Coggeshall—all noted for the manufacture of bays, as above, and for very little else, except I shall make the ladies laugh at the famous old story of the Flitch of Bacon at Dunmow, which is this:

One Robert Fitzwalter, a powerful baron in this county in the time of Henry III., on some merry occasion, which is not preserved in the rest of the story, instituted a custom in the priory here: That whatever married man did not repent of his being married, or quarrel or differ and dispute with his wife within a year and a day after his marriage, and would swear to the truth of it, kneeling upon two hard pointed stones in the churchyard, which stones he caused to be set up in the Priory churchyard for that purpose, the prior and convent, and as many of the town as would, to be present, such person should have a flitch of bacon.

I do not remember to have read that any one ever came to demand it; nor do the people of the place pretend to say, of their own knowledge, that they remember any that did so. A long time ago several did demand it, as they say, but they know not who; neither is there any record of it, nor do they tell us, if it were now to be demanded, who is obliged to deliver the flitch of bacon, the priory being dissolved and gone.

The forest of Epping and Hainault spreads a great part of this country still. I shall speak again of the former in my return from this circuit. Formerly, it is thought, these two forests took up all the west and south part of the county; but particularly we are assured, that it reached to the River Chelmer, and into Dengy Hundred, and from thence again west to Epping and Waltham, where it continues to be a forest still.

Probably this forest of Epping has been a wild or forest ever since this island was inhabited, and may show us, in some parts of it, where enclosures and tillage has not broken in upon it, what the face of this island was before the Romans' time; that is to say, before their landing in Britain.

The constitution of this forest is best seen, I mean as to the antiquity of it, by the merry grant of it from Edward the Confessor before the Norman Conquest to Randolph Peperking, one of his favourites, who was after called Peverell, and whose name remains still in several villages in this county; as particularly that of Hatfield Peverell, in the road from Chelmsford to Witham, which is supposed to be originally a park, which they called a field in those days; and Hartfield may be as much as to say a park for doer; for the stags were in those days called harts, so that this was neither more nor less than Randolph Peperking's Hartfield—that is to say, Ralph Peverell's deer-park.

N.B.—This Ralph Randolph, or Ralph Peverell (call him as you please), had, it seems, a most beautiful lady to his wife, who was daughter of Ingelrick, one of Edward the Confessor's noblemen. He had two sons by her—William Peverell, a famed soldier, and lord or governor of Dover Castle, which he surrendered to William the Conqueror, after the battle in Sussex, and Pain Peverell, his youngest, who was lord of Cambridge. When the eldest son delivered up the castle, the lady, his mother, above named, who was the celebrated beauty of the age, was it seems there, and the Conqueror fell in love with her, and whether by force or by consent, took her away, and she became his mistress, or what else you please to call it. By her he had a son, who was called William, after the Conqueror's Christian name, but retained the name of Peverell, and was afterwards created by the Conqueror lord of Nottingham.

This lady afterwards, as is supposed, by way of penance for her yielding to the Conqueror, founded a nunnery at the village of Hatfield Peverell, mentioned above, and there she lies buried in the chapel of it, which is now the parish church, where her memory is preserved by a tombstone under one of the windows.

Thus we have several towns, where any ancient parks have been placed, called by the name of Hatfield on that very account. As Hatfield Broad Oak in this county, Bishop's Hatfield in Hertfordshire, and several others.

But I return to King Edward's merry way, as I call it, of granting this forest to this Ralph Peperking, which I find in the ancient records, in the very words it was passed in, as follows. Take my explanations with it for the sake of those that are not used to the ancient English:

**The Grant in Old English.**
IChe Edward Koning.
Have given of my Forrest the kepen of the Hundred of Chelmer and Dancing.

To Randolph Peperking, And to his kindling.
With Heorte and Hind, Doe and Bocke,
Hare and Fox, Cat and Brock,
Wild Fowle with his Flock;
Patrich, Pheasant Hen, and Pheasant Cock,
With green and wild Stub and Stock,
To kepen and to yemen with all her might.
Both by Day, and eke by Night;
And Hounds for to hold, Good and Swift and Bold:
Four Greyhound and six Raches,
For Hare and Fox, and Wild Cattes,
And therefore Iche made him my Book.

Witness the Bishop of Wolston. And Booke ylrede many on,

And Sweyne of Essex, our Brother,

And taken him many other
And our steward Howlein, That By sought me for him.

**The Explanation in Modern English.**
I Edward the king,
Have made ranger of my forest of Chelmsford hundred and Deering hundred,

Ralph Peverell, for him and his heirs for ever;
With both the red and fallow deer.
Hare and fox, otter and badger;
Wild fowl of all sorts,
Partridges and pheasants,
Timber and underwood roots and tops;
With power to preserve the forest,
And watch it against deer-stealers and others:
With a right to keep hounds of all sorts,
Four greyhounds and six terriers,
Harriers and foxhounds, and other hounds.
And to this end I have registered this my grant in the crown rolls or books;
To which the bishop has set his hand as a witness for any one to read.
Also signed by the king's brother (or, as some think, the Chancellor Sweyn, then Earl or Count of Essex).
He might call such other witnesses to sign as he thought fit.
Also the king's high steward was a witness, at whose request this grant was obtained of the king.

There are many gentlemen's seats on this side the country, and a great assembly set up at New Hall, near this town, much resorted to by the neighbouring gentry. I shall next proceed to the county of Suffolk, as my first design directed me to do.

From Harwich, therefore, having a mind to view the harbour, I sent my horses round by Manningtree, where there is a timber bridge over the Stour, called Cataway Bridge, and took a boat up the River Orwell for Ipswich. A traveller will hardly understand me, especially a seaman, when I speak of the River Stour and the River Orwell at Harwich, for they know them by no other names than those of Manningtree water and Ipswich water; so while I am on salt water, I must speak as those who use the sea may understand me, and when I am up in the country among the inland towns again, I shall call them out of their names no more.

It is twelve miles from Harwich up the water to Ipswich. Before I come to the town, I must say something of it, because speaking of the river requires it. In former times, that is to say, since the writer of this remembers the place very well, and particularly just before the late Dutch wars, Ipswich was a town of very good business; particularly it was the greatest town in England for large colliers or coal-ships employed between Newcastle and London. Also they built the biggest ships and the best, for the said fetching of coals of any that were employed in that trade. They built, also, there so prodigious strong, that it was an ordinary thing for an Ipswich collier, if no disaster happened to him, to reign (as seamen call it) forty or fifty years, and more.

In the town of Ipswich the masters of these ships generally dwelt, and there were, as they then told me, above a hundred sail of them, belonging to the town at one time, the least of which carried fifteen score, as they compute it, that is, 300 chaldron of coals; this was about the year 1668 (when I first knew the place). This made the town be at that time so populous, for those masters, as they had good ships at sea, so they had large families who lived plentifully, and in very good houses in the town, and several streets were chiefly inhabited by such.

The loss or decay of this trade accounts for the present pretended decay of the town of Ipswich, of which I shall speak more presently. The ships wore out, the masters died off, the trade took a new turn; Dutch flyboats taken in the war, and made free ships by Act of Parliament, thrust themselves into the coal-trade for the interest of the captors, such as the Yarmouth and London merchants, and others; and the Ipswich men dropped gradually out of it, being discouraged by those Dutch flyboats. These Dutch vessels, which cost nothing but the caption, were bought cheap, carried great burthens, and the Ipswich building fell off for want of price, and so the trade decayed, and the town with it. I believe this will be owned for the true beginning of their decay, if I must allow it to be called a decay.

But to return to my passage up the river. In the winter-time those great collier ships, above-mentioned, are always laid up, as they call it; that is to say, the coal trade abates at London, the citizens are generally furnished, their stores taken in, and the demand is over; so that the great ships, the northern seas and coast being also dangerous, the nights long, and the voyage hazardous, go to sea no more, but lie by, the ships are unrigged, the sails, etc., carried ashore, the top-masts struck, and they ride moored in the river, under the advantages and security of sound ground, and a high woody shore, where they lie as safe as in a wet dock; and it was a very agreeable sight to see, perhaps two hundred sail of ships, of all sizes, lie in that posture every winter. All this while, which was usually from Michaelmas to Lady Day, the masters lived calm and secure with their families in Ipswich; and enjoying plentifully, what in the summer they got laboriously at sea, and this made the town of Ipswich very populous in the winter; for as the masters, so most of the men, especially their mates, boatswains, carpenters, etc., were of the same place, and lived in their proportions, just as the masters did; so that in the winter there might be perhaps a thousand men in the town more than in the summer, and perhaps a greater number.

To justify what I advance here, that this town was formerly very full of people, I ask leave to refer to the account of Mr. Camden, and what it was in his time. His words are these:—"Ipswich has a commodious harbour, has been fortified with a ditch and rampart, has a great trade, and is very populous, being adorned with fourteen churches, and large private buildings." This confirms what I have mentioned of the former state of this town; but the present state is my proper work; I therefore return to my voyage up the river.

The sight of these ships thus laid up in the river, as I have said, was very agreeable to me in my passage from Harwich, about five and thirty years before the present journey; and it was in its proportion equally melancholy to hear that there were now scarce forty sail of good colliers that belonged to the whole town.

In a creek in this river, called Lavington Creek, we saw at low water such shoals, or hills rather, of mussels, that great boats might have loaded with them, and no miss have been made of them. Near this creek, Sir Samuel Barnadiston had a very fine seat, as, also, a decoy for wild ducks, and a very noble estate; but it is divided into many branches since the death of the ancient possessor. But I proceed to the town, which is the first in the county of Suffolk of any note this way.

Ipswich is seated, at the distance of twelve miles from Harwich, upon the edge of the river, which, taking a short turn to the west, the town forms, there, a kind of semicircle, or half moon, upon the bank of the river. It is very remarkable, that though ships of 500 ton may, upon a spring tide, come up very near this town, and many ships of that burthen have been built there, yet the river is not navigable any farther than the town itself, or but very little; no, not for the smallest beats; nor does the tide, which rises sometimes thirteen or fourteen feet, and gives them twenty-four feet water very near the town, flow much farther up the river than the town, or not so much as to make it worth speaking of.

He took little notice of the town, or at least of that part of Ipswich, who published in his wild observations on it that ships of 200 ton are built there. I affirm, that I have seen a ship of 400 ton launched at the building-yard, close to the town; and I appeal to the Ipswich colliers (those few that remain) belonging to this town, if several of them carrying seventeen score of coals, which must be upward of 400 ton, have not formerly been built here; but superficial observers must be superficial writers, if they write at all; and to this day, at John's Ness, within a mile and a half of the town itself, ships of any burthen may be built and launched even at neap tides.

I am much mistaken, too, if since the Revolution some very good ships have not been built at this town, and particularly the Melford or Milford galley, a ship of forty guns; as the Greyhound frigate, a man-of-war of thirty-six to forty guns, was at John's Ness. But what is this towards lessening the town of Ipswich, any more than it would be to say, they do not build men-of-war, or East India ships, or ships of five hundred ton burden at St. Catherines, or at Battle Bridge in the Thames? when we know that a mile or two lower, viz., at Radcliffe, Limehouse, or Deptford, they build ships of a thousand ton, and might build first-rate men-of-war too, if there was occasion; and the like might be done in this river of Ipswich, within about two or three miles of the town; so that it would not be at all an out-of-the-way speaking to say, such a ship was built at Ipswich, any more than it is to say, as they do, that the Royal Prince, the great ship lately built for the South Sea Company, was London built, because she was built at Limehouse.

And why then is not Ipswich capable of building and receiving the greatest ships in the navy, seeing they may be built and brought up again laden, within a mile and half of the town?

But the neighbourhood of London, which sucks the vitals of trade in this island to itself, is the chief reason of any decay of business in this place; and I shall, in the course of these observations, hint at it, where many good seaports and large towns, though farther off than Ipswich, and as well fitted for commerce, are yet swallowed up by the immense indraft of trade to the City of London; and more decayed beyond all comparison than Ipswich is supposed to be: as Southampton, Weymouth, Dartmouth, and several others which I shall speak to in their order; and if it be otherwise at this time, with some other towns, which are lately increased in trade and navigation, wealth, and people, while their neighbours decay, it is because they have some particular trade, or accident to trade, which is a kind of nostrum to them, inseparable to the place, and which fixes there by the nature of the thing; as the herring-fishery to Yarmouth; the coal trade to Newcastle; the Leeds clothing trade; the export of butter and lead, and the great corn trade for Holland, is to Hull; the Virginia and West India trade at Liverpool; the Irish trade at Bristol, and the like. Thus the war has brought a flux of business and people, and consequently of wealth, to several places, as well as to Portsmouth, Chatham, Plymouth, Falmouth, and others; and were any wars like those, to continue twenty years with the Dutch, or any nation whose fleets lay that way, as the Dutch do, it would be the like perhaps at Ipswich in a few years, and at other places on the same coast.

But at this present time an occasion offers to speak in favour of this port; namely, the Greenland fishery, lately proposed to be carried on by the South Sea Company. On which account I may freely advance this, without any compliment to the town of Ipswich, no place in Britain is equally qualified like Ipswich; whether we respect the cheapness of building and fitting out their ships and shallops; also furnishing, victualling, and providing them with all kinds of stores; convenience for laying up the ships after the voyage, room for erecting their magazines, warehouses, rope walks, cooperages, etc., on the easiest terms; and especially for the noisome cookery, which attends the boiling their blubber, which may be on this river (as it ought to be) remote from any places of resort. Then their nearness to the market for the oil when it is made, and which, above all, ought to be the chief thing considered in that trade, the easiness of their putting out to sea when they begin their voyage, in which the same wind that carries them from the mouth of the haven, is fair to the very seas of Greenland.

I could say much more to this point if it were needful, and in few words could easily prove, that Ipswich must have the preference of all the port towns of Britain, for being the best centre of the Greenland trade, if ever that trade fall into the management of such a people as perfectly understand, and have a due honest regard to its being managed with the best husbandry, and to the prosperity of the undertaking in general. But whether we shall ever arrive at so happy a time as to recover so useful a trade to our country, which our ancestors had the honour to be the first undertakers of, and which has been lost only through the indolence of others, and the increasing vigilance of our neighbours, that is not my business here to dispute.

What I have said is only to let the world see what improvement this town and port is capable of; I cannot think but that Providence, which made nothing in vain, cannot have reserved so useful, so convenient a port to lie vacant in the world, but that the time will some time or other come (especially considering the improving temper of the present age) when some peculiar beneficial business may be found out, to make the port of Ipswich as useful to the world, and the town as flourishing, as Nature has made it proper and capable to be.

As for the town, it is true, it is but thinly inhabited, in comparison of the extent of it; but to say there are hardly any people to be seen there, is far from being true in fact; and whoever thinks fit to look into the churches and meeting-houses on a Sunday, or other public days, will find there are very great numbers of people there. Or if he thinks fit to view the market, and see how the large shambles, called Cardinal Wolsey's Butchery, are furnished with meat, and the rest of the market stocked with other provisions, must acknowledge that it is not for a few people that all those things are provided. A person very curious, and on whose veracity I think I may depend, going through the market in this town, told me, that he reckoned upwards of six hundred country people on horseback and on foot, with baskets and other carriage, who had all of them brought something or other to town to sell, besides the butchers, and what came in carts and waggons.

It happened to be my lot to be once at this town at the time when a very fine new ship, which was built there for some merchants of London, was to be launched; and if I may give my guess at the numbers of people which appeared on the shore, in the houses, and on the river, I believe I am much within compass if I say there were 20,000 people to see it; but this is only a guess, or they might come a great way to see the sight, or the town may be declined farther since that. But a view of the town is one of the surest rules for a gross estimate.

It is true here is no settled manufacture. The French refugees when they first came over to England began a little to take to this place, and some merchants attempted to set up a linen manufacture in their favour; but it has not met with so much success as was expected, and at present I find very little of it. The poor people are, however, employed, as they are all over these counties, in spinning wool for other towns where manufactures are settled.

The country round Ipswich, as are all the counties so near the coast, is applied chiefly to corn, of which a very great quantity is continually shipped off for London; and sometimes they load corn here for Holland, especially if the market abroad is encouraging. They have twelve parish churches in this town, with three or four meetings; but there are not so many Quakers here as at Colchester, and no Anabaptists or Antipoedo Baptists, that I could hear of—at least, there is no meeting-house of that denomination. There is one meeting-house for the Presbyterians, one for the Independents and one for the Quakers; the first is as large and as fine a building of that kind as most on this side of England, and the inside the best finished of any I have seen, London not excepted; that for the Independents is a handsome new-built building, but not so gay or so large as the other.

There is a great deal of very good company in this town, and though there are not so many of the gentry here as at Bury, yet there are more here than in any other town in the county; and I observed particularly that the company you meet with here are generally persons well informed of the world, and who have something very solid and entertaining in their society. This may happen, perhaps, by their frequent conversing with those who have been abroad, and by their having a remnant of gentlemen and masters of ships among them who have seen more of the world than the people of an inland town are likely to have seen. I take this town to be one of the most agreeable places in England for families who have lived well, but may have suffered in our late calamities of stocks and bubbles, to retreat to, where they may live within their own compass; and several things indeed recommend it to such:—

1. Good houses at very easy rents.

2. An airy, clean, and well-governed town.

3. Very agreeable and improving company almost of every kind.

4. A wonderful plenty of all manner of provisions, whether flesh or fish, and very good of the kind.

5. Those provisions very cheap, so that a family may live cheaper here than in any town in England of its bigness within such a small distance from London.

6. Easy passage to London, either by land or water, the coach going through to London in a day.

The Lord Viscount Hereford has a very fine seat and park in this town; the house indeed is old built, but very commodious; it is called Christ Church, having been, as it is said, a priory or religious house in former times. The green and park is a great addition to the pleasantness of this town, the inhabitants being allowed to divert themselves there with walking, bowling, etc.

The large spire steeple, which formerly stood upon that they call the tower church, was blown down by a great storm of wind many years ago, and in its a fall did much damage to the church.

The government of this town is by two bailiffs, as at Yarmouth. Mr. Camden says they are chosen out of twelve burgesses called portmen, and two justices out of twenty-four more. There has been lately a very great struggle between the two parties for the choice of these two magistrates, which had this amicable conclusion—namely, that they chose one of either side; so that neither party having the victory, it is to be hoped it may be a means to allay the heats and unneighbourly feuds which such things breed in towns so large as this is. They send two members to Parliament, whereof those at this time are Sir William Thompson, Recorder of London, and Colonel Negus, Deputy Master of the Horse to the king.

There are some things very curious to be seen here, however some superficial writers have been ignorant of them. Dr. Beeston, an eminent physician, began a few years ago a physic garden adjoining to his house in this town; and as he is particularly curious, and, as I was told, exquisitely skilled in botanic knowledge, so he has been not only very diligent, but successful too, in making a collection of rare and exotic plants, such as are scarce to be equalled in England.

One Mr. White, a surgeon, resides also in this town. But before I speak of this gentleman, I must observe that I say nothing from personal knowledge; though if I did, I have too good an opinion of his sense to believe he would be pleased with being flattered or complimented in print. But I must be true to matter of fact. This gentleman has begun a collection or chamber of rarities, and with good success too. I acknowledge I had not the opportunity of seeing them; but I was told there are some things very curious in it, as particularly a sea-horse carefully preserved, and perfect in all its parts; two Roman urns full of ashes of human bodies, and supposed to be above 1,700 years old; besides a great many valuable medals and ancient coins. My friend who gave me this account, and of whom I think I may say he speaks without bias, mentions this gentleman, Mr. White, with some warmth as a very valuable person in his particular employ of a surgeon. I only repeat his words. "Mr. White," says he, "to whom the whole town and country are greatly indebted and obliged to pray for his life, is our most skilful surgeon." These, I say, are his own words, and I add nothing to them but this, that it is happy for a town to have such a surgeon, as it is for a surgeon to have such a character.

The country round Ipswich, as if qualified on purpose to accommodate the town for building of ships, is an inexhaustible store-house of timber, of which, now their trade of building ships is abated, they send very great quantities to the king's building-yards at Chatham, which by water is so little a way that they often run to it from the mouth of the river at Harwich in one tide.

From Ipswich I took a turn into the country to Hadleigh, principally to satisfy my curiosity and see the place where that famous martyr and pattern of charity and religious zeal in Queen Mary's time, Dr. Rowland Taylor, was put to death. The inhabitants, who have a wonderful veneration for his memory, show the very place where the stake which he was bound to was set up, and they have put a stone upon it which nobody will remove; but it is a more lasting monument to him that he lives in the hearts of the people—I say more lasting than a tomb of marble would be, for the memory of that good man will certainly never be out of the poor people's minds as long as this island shall retain the Protestant religion among them. How long that may be, as things are going, and if the detestable conspiracy of the Papists now on foot should succeed, I will not pretend to say.

A little to the left is Sudbury, which stands upon the River Stour, mentioned above—a river which parts the counties of Suffolk and Essex, and which is within these few years made navigable to this town, though the navigation does not, it seems, answer the charge, at least not to advantage.

I know nothing for which this town is remarkable, except for being very populous and very poor. They have a great manufacture of says and perpetuanas, and multitudes of poor people are employed in working them; but the number of the poor is almost ready to eat up the rich. However, this town sends two members to Parliament, though it is under no form of government particularly to itself other than as a village, the head magistrate whereof is a constable.

Near adjoining to it is a village called Long Melfort, and a very long one it is, from which I suppose it had that addition to its name; it is full of very good houses, and, as they told me, is richer, and has more wealthy masters of the manufacture in it, than in Sudbury itself.

Here and in the neighbourhood are some ancient families of good note; particularly here is a fine dwelling, the ancient seat of the Cordells, whereof Sir William Cordell was Master of the Rolls in the time of Queen Elizabeth; but the family is now extinct, the last heir, Sir John Cordell, being killed by a fall from his horse, died unmarried, leaving three sisters co-heiresses to a very noble estate, most of which, if not all, is now centred on the only surviving sister, and with her in marriage is given to Mr. Firebrass, eldest son of Sir Basil Firebrass, formerly a flourishing merchant in London, but reduced by many disasters. His family now rises by the good fortune of his son, who proves to be a gentleman of very agreeable parts, and well esteemed in the country.

From this part of the country, I returned north-west by Lenham, to visit St. Edmund's Bury, a town of which other writers have talked very largely, and perhaps a little too much. It is a town famed for its pleasant situation and wholesome air, the Montpelier of Suffolk, and perhaps of England. This must be attributed to the skill of the monks of those times, who chose so beautiful a situation for the seat of their retirement; and who built here the greatest and, in its time, the most flourishing monastery in all these parts of England, I mean the monastery of St. Edmund the Martyr. It was, if we believe antiquity, a house of pleasure in more ancient times, or to speak more properly, a court of some of the Saxon or East Angle kings; and, as Mr. Camden says, was even then called a royal village, though it much better merits that name now; it being the town of all this part of England, in proportion to its bigness, most thronged with gentry, people of the best fashion, and the most polite conversation. This beauty and healthiness of its situation was no doubt the occasion which drew the clergy to settle here, for they always chose the best places in the country to build in, either for richness of soil, or for health and pleasure in the situation of their religious houses.

For the like reason, I doubt not, they translated the bones of the martyred king St. Edmund to this place; for it is a vulgar error to say he was murdered here. His martyrdom, it is plain, was at Hoxon or Henilsdon, near Harlston, on the Waveney, in the farthest northern verge of the county; but Segebert, king of the East Angles, had built a religions house in this pleasant rich part of the county; and as the monks began to taste the pleasure of the place, they procured the body of this saint to be removed hither, which soon increased the wealth and revenues of their house, by the zeal of that day, in going on pilgrimage to the shrine of the blessed St. Edmund.

We read, however, that after this the Danes, under King Sweno, over-running this part of the country, destroyed this monastery and burnt it to the ground, with the church and town. But see the turn religion gives to things in the world; his son, King Canutus, at first a Pagan and a tyrant, and the most cruel ravager of all that crew, coming to turn Christian, and being touched in conscience for the soul of his father, in having robbed God and his holy martyr St. Edmund, sacrilegiously destroying the church, and plundering the monastery; I say, touched with remorse, and, as the monks pretend, terrified with a vision of St. Edmund appearing to him, he rebuilt the house, the church, and the town also, and very much added to the wealth of the abbot and his fraternity, offering his crown at the feet of St. Edmund, giving the house to the monks, town and all; so that they were absolute lords of the town, and governed it by their steward for many ages. He also gave them a great many good lordships, which they enjoyed till the general suppression of abbeys, in the time of Henry VIII.

But I am neither writing the history or searching the antiquity of the abbey, or town; my business is the present state of the place.

The abbey is demolished; its ruins are all that is to be seen of its glory: out of the old building, two very beautiful churches are built, and serve the two parishes, into which the town is divided, and they stand both in one churchyard. Here it was, in the path-way between these two churches, that a tragical and almost unheard-of act of barbarity was committed, which made the place less pleasant for some time than it used to be, when Arundel Coke, Esq., a barrister-at-law, of a very ancient family, attempted, with the assistance of a barbarous assassin, to murder in cold blood, and in the arms of hospitality, Edward Crisp, Esq., his brother-in-law, leading him out from his own house, where he had invited him, his wife and children, to supper; I say, leading him out in the night, on pretence of going to see some friend that was known to them both; but in this churchyard, giving a signal to the assassin he had hired, he attacked him with a hedge-bill, and cut him, as one might say, almost in pieces; and when they did not doubt of his being dead, they left him. His head and face was so mangled, that it may be said to be next to a miracle that he was not quite killed: yet so Providence directed for the exemplary punishment of the assassins, that the gentleman recovered to detect them, who (though he outlived the assault) were both executed as they deserved, and Mr. Crisp is yet alive. They were condemned on the statute for defacing and dismembering, called the Coventry Act.

But this accident does not at all lessen the pleasure and agreeable delightful show of the town of Bury; it is crowded with nobility and gentry, and all sorts of the most agreeable company; and as the company invites, so there is the appearance of pleasure upon the very situation; and they that live at Bury are supposed to live there for the sake of it.

The Lord Jermin, afterwards Lord Dover, and, since his lordship's decease, Sir Robert Davers, enjoyed the most delicious seat of Rushbrook, near this town.

The present members of Parliament for this place are Jermyn Davers and James Reynolds, Esquires.

Mr. Harvey, afterwards created Lord Harvey, by King William, and since that made Earl of Bristol by King George, lived many years in this town, leaving a noble and pleasantly situated house in Lincolnshire, for the more agreeable living on a spot so completely qualified for a life of delight as this of Bury.

The Duke of Grafton, now Lord-Lieutenant of Ireland, has also a stately house at Euston, near this town, which he enjoys in right of his mother, daughter to the Earl of Arlington, one of the chief ministers of State in the reign of King Charles II., and who made the second letter in the word "cabal," a word formed by that famous satirist Andrew Marvell, to represent the five heads of the politics of that time, as the word "smectymnus" was on a former occasion.

I shall believe nothing so scandalous of the ladies of this town and the country round it as a late writer insinuates. That the ladies round the country appear mighty gay and agreeable at the time of the fair in this town I acknowledge; one hardly sees such a show in any part of the world; but to suggest they come hither, as to a market, is so coarse a jest, that the gentlemen that wait on them hither (for they rarely come but in good company) ought to resent and correct him for it.

It is true, Bury Fair, like Bartholomew Fair, is a fair for diversion, more than for trade; and it may be a fair for toys and for trinkets, which the ladies may think fit to lay out some of their money in, as they see occasion. But to judge from thence that the knights' daughters of Norfolk, Cambridgeshire, and Suffolk—that is to say, for it cannot be understood any otherwise, the daughters of all the gentry of the three counties—come hither to be picked up, is a way of speaking I never before heard any author have the assurance to make use of in print.

The assembly he justly commends for the bright appearance of the beauties; but with a sting in the tail of this compliment, where he says they seldom end without some considerable match or intrigue; and yet he owns that during the fair these assemblies are held every night. Now that these fine ladies go intriguing every night, and that too after the comedy is done, which is after the fair and raffling is over for the day, so that it must be very late. This is a terrible character for the ladies of Bury, and intimates, in short, that most of them are loose women, which is a horrid abuse upon the whole country.

Now, though I like not the assemblies at all, and shall in another place give them something of their due, yet having the opportunity to see the fair at Bury, and to see that there were, indeed, abundance of the finest ladies, or as fine as any in Britain, yet I must own the number of the ladies at the comedy, or at the assembly, is no way equal to the number that are seen in the town, much less are they equal to the whole body of the ladies in the three counties; and I must also add, that though it is far from true that all that appear at the assembly are there for matches or intrigues, yet I will venture to say that they are not the worst of the ladies who stay away, neither are they the fewest in number or the meanest in beauty, but just the contrary; and I do not at all doubt, but that the scandalous liberty some take at those assemblies will in time bring them out of credit with the virtuous part of the sex here, as it has done already in Kent and other places, and that those ladies who most value their reputation will be seen less there than they have been; for though the institution of them has been innocent and virtuous, the ill use of them, and the scandalous behaviour of some people at them, will in time arm virtue against them, and they will be laid down as they have been set up without much satisfaction.

But the beauty of this town consists in the number of gentry who dwell in and near it, the polite conversation among them, the affluence and plenty they live in, the sweet air they breathe in, and the pleasant country they have to go abroad in.

Here is no manufacturing in this town, or but very little, except spinning, the chief trade of the place depending upon the gentry who live there, or near it, and who cannot fail to cause trade enough by the expense of their families and equipages among the people of a county town. They have but a very small river, or rather but a very small branch of a small river, at this town, which runs from hence to Milden Hall, on the edge of the fens. However, the town and gentlemen about have been at the charge, or have so encouraged the engineer who was at the charge, that they have made this river navigable to the said Milden Hall, from whence there is a navigable dyke, called Milden Hall Drain, which goes into the River Ouse, and so to Lynn; so that all their coal and wine, iron, lead, and other heavy goods, are brought by water from Lynn, or from London, by the way of Lynn, to the great ease of the tradesmen.

This town is famous for two great events. One was that in the year 1447, in the 25th year of Henry VI., a Parliament was held here.

The other was, that at the meeting of this Parliament, the great Humphrey, Duke of Gloucester, regent of the kingdom during the absence of King Henry V. and the minority of Henry VI., and to his last hour the safeguard of the whole nation, and darling of the people, was basely murdered here; by whose death the gate was opened to that dreadful war between the houses of Lancaster and York, which ended in the confusion of that very race who are supposed to have contrived that murder.

From St. Edmund's Bury I returned by Stowmarket and Needham to Ipswich, that I might keep as near the coast as was proper to my designed circuit or journey; and from Ipswich, to visit the sea again, I went to Woodbridge, and from thence to Orford, on the sea side.

Woodbridge has nothing remarkable, but that it is a considerable market for butter and corn to be exported to London; for now begins that part which is ordinarily called High Suffolk, which, being a rich soil, is for a long tract of ground wholly employed in dairies, and they again famous for the best butter, and perhaps the worst cheese, in England. The butter is barrelled, or often pickled up in small casks, and sold, not in London only, but I have known a firkin of Suffolk butter sent to the West Indies, and brought back to England again, and has been perfectly good and sweet, as at first.

The port for the shipping off their Suffolk butter is chiefly Woodbridge, which for that reason is full of corn factors and butter factors, some of whom are very considerable merchants.

From hence, turning down to the shore, we see Orfordness, a noted point of land for the guide of the colliers and coasters, and a good shelter for them to ride under when a strong north-east wind blows and makes a foul shore on the coast.

South of the Ness is Orford Haven, being the mouth of two little rivers meeting together. It is a very good harbour for small vessels, but not capable of receiving a ship of burden.

Orford was once a good town, but is decayed, and as it stands on the land side of the river the sea daily throws up more land to it, and falls off itself from it, as if it was resolved to disown the place, and that it should be a seaport no longer.

A little farther lies Aldborough, as thriving, though without a port, as the other is decaying, with a good river in the front of it.

There are some gentlemen's seats up farther from the sea, but very few upon the coast.

From Aldborough to Dunwich there are no towns of note; even this town seems to be in danger of being swallowed up, for fame reports that once they had fifty churches in the town; I saw but one left, and that not half full of people.

This town is a testimony of the decay of public things, things of the most durable nature; and as the old poet expresses it,

"By numerous examples we may see,
That towns and cities die as well as we."

The ruins of Carthage, of the great city of Jerusalem, or of ancient Rome, are not at all wonderful to me. The ruins of Nineveh, which are so entirely sunk as that it is doubtful where the city stood; the ruins of Babylon, or the great Persepolis, and many capital cities, which time and the change of monarchies have overthrown, these, I say, are not at all wonderful, because being the capitals of great and flourishing kingdoms, where those kingdoms were overthrown, the capital cities necessarily fell with them; but for a private town, a seaport, and a town of commerce, to decay, as it were, of itself (for we never read of Dunwich being plundered or ruined by any disaster, at least, not of late years); this, I must confess, seems owing to nothing but to the fate of things, by which we see that towns, kings, countries, families, and persons, have all their elevation, their medium, their declination, and even their destruction in the womb of time, and the course of nature. It is true, this town is manifestly decayed by the invasion of the waters, and as other towns seem sufferers by the sea, or the tide withdrawing from their ports, such as Orford, just now named, Winchelsea in Kent, and the like, so this town is, as it were, eaten up by the sea, as above; and the still encroaching ocean seems to threaten it with a fatal immersion in a few years more.

Yet Dunwich, however ruined, retains some share of trade, as particularly for the shipping of butter, cheese, and corn, which is so great a business in this county, that it employs a great many people and ships also; and this port lies right against the particular part of the county for butter, as Framlingham, Halstead, etc. Also a very great quantity of corn is bought up hereabout for the London market; for I shall still touch that point how all the counties in England contribute something towards the subsistence of the great city of London, of which the butter here is a very considerable article; as also coarse cheese, which I mentioned before, used chiefly for the king's ships.

Hereabouts they begin to talk of herrings and the fishery; and we find in the ancient records that this town, which was then equal to a large city, paid, among other tribute to the government, fifty thousand of herrings. Here also, and at Swole, or Southole, the next seaport, they cure sprats in the same manner as they do herrings at Yarmouth; that is to say, speaking in their own language, they make red sprats; or to speak good English, they make sprats red.

It is remarkable that this town is now so much washed away by the sea, that what little trade they have is carried on by Walderswick, a little town near Swole, the vessels coming in there, because the ruins of

Dunwich make the shore there unsafe and uneasy to the boats; from whence the northern coasting seamen a rude verse of their own using, and I suppose of their own making, as follows,

"Swoul and Dunwich, and Walderswick,
All go in at one lousie creek."

This "lousie creek," in short, is a little river at Swoul, which our late famous atlas-maker calls a good harbour for ships, and rendezvous of the royal navy; but that by-the-bye; the author, it seems, knew no better.

From Dunwich we came to Southwold, the town above-named: this is a small port town upon the coast, at the mouth of a little river called the Blith. I found no business the people here were employed in but the fishery, as above, for herrings and sprats, which they cure by the help of smoke, as they do at Yarmouth.

There is but one church in this town, but it is a very large one and well built, as most of the churches in this county are, and of impenetrable flint; indeed, there is no occasion for its being so large, for staying there one Sabbath day, I was surprised to see an extraordinary large church, capable of receiving five or six thousand people, and but twenty-seven in it besides the parson and the clerk; but at the same time the meeting-house of the Dissenters was full to the very doors, having, as I guessed, from six to eight hundred people in it.

This town is made famous for a very great engagement at sea, in the year 1672, between the English and Dutch fleets, in the bay opposite to the town, in which, not to be partial to ourselves, the English fleet was worsted; and the brave Montague, Earl of Sandwich, Admiral under the Duke of York, lost his life. The ship Royal Prince, carrying one hundred guns, in which he was, and which was under him, commanded by Sir Edward Spragg, was burnt, and several other ships lost, and about six hundred seamen; part of those killed in the fight were, as I was told, brought on shore here and buried in the churchyard of this town, as others also were at Ipswich.

At this town in particular, and so at all the towns on this coast, from Orfordness to Yarmouth, is the ordinary place where our summer friends the swallows first land when they come to visit us; and here they may be said to embark for their return, when they go back into warmer climates; and as I think the following remark, though of so trifling a circumstance, may be both instructing as well as diverting, it may be very proper in this place. The case is this; I was some years before at this place, at the latter end of the year, viz., about the beginning of October, and lodging in a house that looked into the churchyard, I observed in the evening, an unusual multitude of birds sitting on the leads of the church. Curiosity led me to go nearer to see what they were, and I found they were all swallows; that there was such an infinite number that they covered the whole roof of the church, and of several houses near, and perhaps might of more houses which I did not see. This led me to inquire of a grave gentleman whom I saw near me, what the meaning was of such a prodigious multitude of swallows sitting there. "Oh, sir," says he, turning towards the sea, "you may see the reason; the wind is off sea." I did not seem fully informed by that expression, so he goes on, "I perceive, sir," says he, "you are a stranger to it; you must then understand first, that this is the season of the year when the swallows, their food here failing, begin to leave us, and return to the country, wherever it be, from whence I suppose they came; and this being the nearest to the coast of Holland, they come here to embark" (this he said smiling a little); "and now, sir," says he, "the weather being too calm or the wind contrary, they are waiting for a gale, for they are all wind-bound."

This was more evident to me, when in the morning I found the wind had come about to the north-west in the night, and there was not one swallow to be seen of near a million, which I believe was there the night before.

How those creatures know that this part of the Island of Great Britain is the way to their home, or the way that they are to go; that this very point is the nearest cut over, or even that the nearest cut is best for them, that we must leave to the naturalists to determine, who insist upon it that brutes cannot think.

Certain it is that the swallows neither come hither for warm weather nor retire from cold; the thing is of quite another nature. They, like the shoals of fish in the sea, pursue their prey; they are a voracious creature, they feed flying; their food is found in the air, viz., the insects, of which in our summer evenings, in damp and moist places, the air is full. They come hither in the summer because our air is fuller of fogs and damps than in other countries, and for that reason feeds great quantities of insects. If the air be hot and dry the gnats die of themselves, and even the swallows will be found famished for want, and fall down dead out of the air, their food being taken from them. In like manner, when cold weather comes in the insects all die, and then of necessity the swallows quit us, and follow their food wherever they go. This they do in the manner I have mentioned above, for sometimes they are seen to go off in vast flights like a cloud. And sometimes again, when the wind grows fair, they go away a few and a few as they come, not staying at all upon the coast.

Note.—This passing and re-passing of the swallows is observed nowhere so much, that I have heard of, or in but few other places, except on this eastern coast, namely, from above Harwich to the east point of Norfolk, called Winterton Ness, North, which is all right against Holland. We know nothing of them any farther north, the passage of the sea being, as I suppose, too broad from Flamborough Head and the shore of Holderness in Yorkshire, etc.

I find very little remarkable on this side of Suffolk, but what is on the sea-shore as above. The inland country is that which they properly call High Suffolk, and is full of rich feeding grounds and large farms, mostly employed in dairies for making the Suffolk butter and cheese, of which I have spoken already. Among these rich grounds stand some market towns, though not of very considerable note; such as Framlingham, where was once a royal castle, to which Queen Mary retired when the Northumberland faction, in behalf of the Lady Jane, endeavoured to supplant her. And it was this part of Suffolk where the Gospellers, as they were then called, preferred their loyalty to their religion, and complimented the Popish line at expense of their share of the Reformation. But they paid dear for it, and their successors have learned better politics since.

In these parts are also several good market towns, some in this county and some in the other, as Beccles, Bungay, Harlston, etc., all on the edge of the River Waveney, which parts here the counties of Suffolk and Norfolk. And here in a bye-place, and out of common remark, lies the ancient town of Hoxon, famous for being the place where St. Edmund was martyred, for whom so many cells and shrines have been set up and monasteries built, and in honour of whom the famous monastery of St. Edmundsbury, above mentioned, was founded, which most people erroneously think was the place where the said murder was committed.

Besides the towns mentioned above, there are Halesworth, Saxmundham, Debenham, Aye, or Eye, all standing in this eastern side of Suffolk, in which, as I have said, the whole country is employed in dairies or in feeding of cattle.

This part of England is also remarkable for being the first where the feeding and fattening of cattle, both sheep as well as black cattle, with turnips, was first practised in England, which is made a very great part of the improvement of their lands to this day, and from whence the practice is spread over most of the east and south parts of England to the great enriching of the farmers and increase of fat cattle. And though some have objected against the goodness of the flesh thus fed with turnips, and have fancied it would taste of the root, yet upon experience it is found that at market there is no difference, nor can they that buy single out one joint of mutton from another by the taste. So that the complaint which our nice palates at first made begins to cease of itself, and a very great quantity of beef and mutton also is brought every year and every week to London from this side of England, and much more than was formerly known to be fed there.

I cannot omit, however little it may seem, that this county of Suffolk is particularly famous for furnishing the City of London and all the counties round with turkeys, and that it is thought there are more turkeys bred in this county and the part of Norfolk that adjoins to it than in all the rest of England, especially for sale, though this may be reckoned, as I say above, but a trifling thing to take notice of in these remarks; yet, as I have hinted, that I shall observe how London is in general supplied with all its provisions from the whole body of the nation, and how every part of the island is engaged in some degree or other of that supply. On this account I could not omit it, nor will it be found so inconsiderable an article as some may imagine, if this be true, which I received an account of from a person living on the place, viz., that they have counted three hundred droves of turkeys (for they drive them all in droves on foot) pass in one season over Stratford Bridge on the River Stour, which parts Suffolk from Essex, about six miles from Colchester, on the road from Ipswich to London. These droves, as they say, generally contain from three hundred to a thousand each drove; so that one may suppose them to contain five hundred one with another, which is one hundred and fifty thousand in all; and yet this is one of the least passages, the numbers which travel by Newmarket Heath and the open country and the forest, and also the numbers that come by Sudbury and Clare being many more.

For the further supplies of the markets of London with poultry, of which these countries particularly abound, they have within these few years found it practicable to make the geese travel on foot too, as well as the turkeys, and a prodigious number are brought up to London in droves from the farthest parts of Norfolk; even from the fen country about Lynn, Downham, Wisbech, and the Washes; as also from all the east side of Norfolk and Suffolk, of whom it is very frequent now to meet droves with a thousand, sometimes two thousand in a drove. They begin to drive them generally in August, by which time the harvest is almost over, and the geese may feed in the stubbles as they go. Thus they hold on to the end of October, when the roads begin to be too stiff and deep for their broad feet and short legs to march in.

Besides these methods of driving these creatures on foot, they have of late also invented a new method of carriage, being carts formed on purpose, with four stories or stages to put the creatures in one above another, by which invention one cart will carry a very great number; and for the smoother going they drive with two horses abreast, like a coach, so quartering the road for the ease of the gentry that thus ride. Changing horses, they travel night and day, so that they bring the fowls seventy, eighty, or, one hundred miles in two days and one night. The horses in this new-fashioned voiture go two abreast, as above, but no perch below, as in a coach, but they are fastened together by a piece of wood lying crosswise upon their necks, by which they are kept even and together, and the driver sits on the top of the cart like as in the public carriages for the army, etc.

In this manner they hurry away the creatures alive, and infinite numbers are thus carried to London every year. This method is also particular for the carrying young turkeys or turkey poults in their season, which are valuable, and yield a good price at market; as also for live chickens in the dear seasons, of all which a very great number are brought in this manner to London, and more prodigiously out of this country than any other part of England, which is the reason of my speaking of it here.

In this part, which we call High Suffolk, there are not so many families of gentry or nobility placed as in the other side of the country. But it is observed that though their seats are not so frequent here, their estates are; and the pleasure of West Suffolk is much of it supported by the wealth of High Suffolk, for the richness of the lands and application of the people to all kinds of improvement is scarce credible; also the farmers are so very considerable and their farms and dairies so large that it is very frequent for a farmer to have £1,000 stock upon his farm in cows only.

NORFOLK.

From High Suffolk I passed the Waveney into Norfolk, near Schole Inn. In my passage I saw at Redgrave (the seat of the family) a most exquisite monument of Sir John Holt, Knight, late Lord Chief Justice of the King's Bench several years, and one of the most eminent lawyers of his time. One of the heirs of the family is now building a fine seat about a mile on the south side of Ipswich, near the road.

The epitaph or inscription on this monument is as follows:—

M. S.
D. Johannis Holt, Equitis Aur.
Totius Angliæ in Banco Regis
per 21 Annos continuos
Capitalis Justitiarii
Gulielmo Regi Annæqur Reginæ
Consiliarii perpetui:
Libertatis ac Legum Anglicarum
Assertoris, Vindicis, Custodis,
Vigilis Acris & intrepidi,
Rolandus Frater Uncius & Hæres
Optime de se Merito posuit,
Die Martis Vto. 1709. Sublatus est
ex Oculis nostris
Natus 30 Decembris, Anno 1642.

When we come into Norfolk, we see a face of diligence spread over the whole country; the vast manufactures carried on (in chief) by the Norwich weavers employs all the country round in spinning yarn for them; besides many thousand packs of yarn which they receive from other countries, even from as far as Yorkshire and Westmoreland, of which I shall speak in its place.

This side of Norfolk is very populous, and thronged with great and spacious market-towns, more and larger than any other part of England so far from London, except Devonshire, and the West Riding of Yorkshire; for example, between the frontiers of Suffolk and the city of Norwich on this side, which is not above 22 miles in breadth, are the following market-towns, viz.:—

| | | |
|---|---|---|
| Thetford, | Hingham, | Harleston, |
| Diss, | West Dereham, | E. Dereham, |
| Harling, | Attleborough, | Watton, |
| Bucknam, | Windham, | Loddon, etc. |

Most of these towns are very populous and large; but that which is most remarkable is, that the whole country round them is so interspersed with villages, and those villages so large, and so full of people, that they are equal to market-towns in other countries; in a word, they render this eastern part of Norfolk exceeding full of inhabitants.

An eminent weaver of Norwich gave me a scheme of their trade on this occasion, by which, calculating from the number of looms at that time employed in the city of Norwich only, besides those employed in other towns in the same county, he made it appear very plain, that there were 120,000 people employed in the woollen and silk and wool manufactures of that city only; not that the people all lived in the city, though Norwich is a very large and populous city too: but, I say, they were employed for spinning the yarn used for such goods as were all made in that city. This account is curious enough, and very exact, but it is too long for the compass of this work.

This shows the wonderful extent of the Norwich manufacture, or stuff-weaving trade, by which so many thousands of families are maintained. Their trade, indeed, felt a very sensible decay, and the cries of the poor began to be very loud, when the wearing of painted calicoes was grown to such a height in England, as was seen about two or three years ago; but an Act of Parliament having been obtained, though not without great struggle, in the years 1720 and 1721, for prohibiting the use and wearing of calicoes, the stuff trade revived incredibly; and as I passed this part of the country in the year 1723, the manufacturers assured me that there was not, in all the eastern and middle part of Norfolk, any hand unemployed, if they would work; and that the very children, after four or five years of age, could every one earn their own bread. But I return to speak of the villages and towns in the rest of the county; I shall come to the city of Norwich by itself.

This throng of villages continues through all the east part of the country, which is of the greatest extent, and where the manufacture is chiefly carried on. If any part of it be waste and thin of inhabitants, it is the west part, drawing a line from about Brand, or Brandon, south, to Walsinghan, north. This part of the country indeed is full of open plains, and somewhat sandy and barren, and feeds great flocks of good sheep; but put it all together, the county of Norfolk has the most people in the least tract of land of any county in England, except about London, and Exon, and the West Riding of Yorkshire, as above.

Add to this, that there is no single county in England, except as above, that can boast of three towns so populous, so rich, and so famous for trade and navigation, as in this county. By these three towns, I mean the city of Norwich, the towns of Yarmouth and Lynn. Besides that, it has several other seaports of very good trade, as Wisbech, Wells, Burnham, Clye, etc.

Norwich is the capital of all the county, and the centre of all the trade and manufactures which I have just mentioned; an ancient, large, rich, and populous city. If a stranger was only to ride through or view the city of Norwich for a day, he would have much more reason to think there was a town without inhabitants, than there is really to say so of Ipswich; but on the contrary if he was to view the city, either on a Sabbath-day, or on any public occasion, he would wonder where all the people could dwell, the multitude is so great. But the case is this: the inhabitants being all busy at their manufactures, dwell in their garrets at their looms, and in their combing shops (so they call them), twisting-mills, and other work-houses, almost all the works they are employed in being done within doors. There are in this city thirty-two parishes besides the cathedral, and a great many meeting-houses of Dissenters of all denominations. The public edifices are chiefly the castle, ancient and decayed, and now for many years past made use of for a gaol. The Duke of Norfolk's house was formerly kept well, and the gardens preserved for the pleasure and diversion of the citizens, but since feeling too sensibly the sinking circumstances of that once glorious family, who were the first peers and hereditary earl-marshals of England.

The walls of this city are reckoned three miles in circumference, taking in more ground than the City of London, but much of that ground lying open in pasture-fields and gardens; nor does it seem to be, like some ancient places, a decayed, declining town, and that the walls mark out its ancient dimensions; for we do not see room to suppose that it was ever larger or more populous than it is now. But the walls seem to be placed as if they expected that the city would in time increase sufficiently to fill them up with buildings.

The cathedral of this city is a fine fabric, and the spire steeple very high and beautiful. It is not ancient, the bishop's see having been first at Thetford, from whence it was not translated hither till the twelfth century. Yet the church has so many antiquities in it, that our late great scholar and physician, Sir Thomas Brown, thought it worth his while to write a whole book to collect the monuments and inscriptions in this church, to which I refer the reader.

The River Yare runs through this city, and is navigable thus far without the help of any art (that is to say, without locks or stops), and being increased by other waters, passes afterwards through a long tract of the richest meadows, and the largest, take them all together, that are anywhere in England, lying for thirty miles in length, from this city to Yarmouth, including the return of the said meadows on the bank of the Waveney south, and on the River Thyrn north.

Here is one thing indeed strange in itself, and more so, in that history seems to be quite ignorant of the occasion of it. The River Waveney is a considerable river, and of a deep and full channel, navigable for large barges as high as Beccles; it runs for a course of about fifty miles, between the two counties of Suffolk and Norfolk, as a boundary to both; and pushing on, though with a gentle stream, towards the sea, no one would doubt, but, that when they see the river growing broader and deeper, and going directly towards the sea, even to the edge of the beach—that is to say, within a mile of the main ocean—no stranger, I say, but would expect to see its entrance into the sea at that place, and a noble harbour for ships at the mouth of it; when on a sudden, the land rising high by the seaside, crosses the head of the river, like a dam, checks the whole course of it, and it returns, bending its course west, for two miles, or thereabouts; and then turning north, through another long course of meadows (joining to those just now mentioned) seeks out the River Yare, that it may join its water with hers, and find their way to the sea together.

Some of our historians tell a long, fabulous story of this river being once open, and a famous harbour for ships belonging to a town of Lowestoft adjoining; but that the town of Yarmouth envying the prosperity of the said town of Lowestoft, made war upon them; and that after many bloody battles, as well by sea as by land, they came at last to a decisive action at sea with their respective fleets, and the victory fell to the Yarmouth men, the Lowestoft fleet being overthrown and utterly destroyed; and that upon this victory, the Yarmouth men either actually did stop up the mouth of the said river, or obliged the vanquished Lowestoft men to do it themselves, and bound them never to attempt to open it again.

I believe my share of this story, and I recommend no more of it to the reader; adding, that I see no authority for the relation, neither do the relators agree either in the time of it, or in the particulars of the fact; that is to say, in whose reign, or under what government all this happened; in what year, and the like; so I satisfy myself with transcribing the matter of fact, and then leave it as I find it.

In this vast tract of meadows are fed a prodigious number of black cattle which are said to be fed up for the fattest beef, though not the largest in England; and the quantity is so great, as that they not only supply the city of Norwich, the town of Yarmouth, and county adjacent, but send great quantities of them weekly in all the winter season to London.

And this in particular is worthy remark, that the gross of all the Scots cattle which come yearly into England are brought hither, being brought to a small village lying north of the city of Norwich, called St. Faith's, where the Norfolk graziers go and buy them.

These Scots runts, so they call them, coming out of the cold and barren mountains of the Highlands in Scotland, feed so eagerly on the rich pasture in these marshes, that they thrive in an unusual manner, and grow monstrously fat; and the beef is so delicious for taste, that the inhabitants prefer them to the English cattle, which are much larger and fairer to look at; and they may very well do so. Some have told me, and I believe with good judgment, that there are above forty thousand of these Scots cattle fed in this county every year, and most of them in the said marshes between Norwich, Beccles, and Yarmouth.

Yarmouth is an ancient town, much older than Norwich; and at present, though not standing on so much ground, yet better built; much more complete; for number of inhabitants, not much inferior; and for wealth, trade, and advantage of its situation, infinitely superior to Norwich.

It is placed on a peninsula between the River Yare and the sea; the two last lying parallel to one another, and the town in the middle. The river lies on the west side of the town, and being grown very large and deep, by a conflux of all the rivers on this side the county, forms the haven; and the town facing to the west also, and open to the river, makes the finest quay in England, if not in Europe, not inferior even to that of Marseilles itself.

The ships ride here so close, and, as it were, keeping up one another, with their headfasts on shore, that for half a mile together they go across the stream with their bowsprits over the land, their bows, or heads touching the very wharf; so that one may walk from ship to ship as on a floating bridge, all along by the shore-side. The quay reaching from the drawbridge almost to the south gate, is so spacious and wide, that in some places it is near one hundred yards from the houses to the wharf. In this pleasant and agreeable range of houses are some very magnificent buildings, and among the rest, the Custom House and Town Hall, and some merchant's houses, which look like little palaces rather than the dwelling-houses of private men.

The greatest defect of this beautiful town seems to be that, though it is very rich and increasing in wealth and trade, and consequently in people, there is not room to enlarge the town by building, which would be certainly done much more than it is, but that the river on the land side prescribes them, except at the north end without the gate; and even there the land is not very agreeable. But had they had a larger space within the gates there would before now have been many spacious streets of noble fine buildings erected, as we see is done in some other thriving towns in England, as at Liverpool, Manchester, Bristol, Frome, etc.

The quay and the harbour of this town during the fishing fair, as they call it, which is every Michaelmas, one sees the land covered with people, and the river with barques and boats, busy day and night landing and carrying of the herrings, which they catch here in such prodigious quantities, that it is incredible. I happened to be there during their fishing fair, when I told in one tide 110 barques and fishing vessels coming up the river all laden with herrings, and all taken the night before; and this was besides what was brought on shore on the Dean (that is the seaside of the town) by open boats, which they call cobles, and which often bring in two or three last of fish at a time. The barques often bring in ten last a piece.

This fishing fair begins on Michaelmas Day, and lasts all the month of October, by which time the herrings draw off to sea, shoot their spawn, and are no more fit for the merchant's business—at least, not those that are taken thereabouts.

The quantity of herrings that are caught in this season are diversely accounted for. Some have said that the towns of Yarmouth and Lowestoft only have taken 40,000 last in a season. I will not venture to confirm that report; but this I have heard the merchants themselves say, viz., that they have cured—that is to say, hanged and dried in the smoke—40,000 barrels of merchantable red herrings in one season, which is in itself (though far short of the other) yet a very considerable article; and it is to be added that this is besides all the herrings consumed in the country towns of both those populous counties for thirty miles from the sea, whither very great quantities are carried every tide during the whole season.

But this is only one branch of the great trade carried on in this town. Another part of this commerce is in the exporting these herrings after they are cured; and for this their merchants have a great trade to Genoa, Leghorn, Naples, Messina, and Venice; as also to Spain and Portugal, also exporting with their herring very great quantities of worsted stuffs, and stuffs made of silk and worsted, camblets, etc., the manufactures of the neighbouring city of Norwich and of the places adjacent.

Besides this, they carry on a very considerable trade with Holland, whose opposite neighbours they are; and a vast quantity of woollen manufactures they export to the Dutch every year. Also they have a fishing trade to the North Seas for white fish, which from the place are called the North Sea cod.

They have also a considerable trade to Norway and to the Baltic, from whence they bring back deals and fir timber, oaken plank, balks, spars, oars, pitch, tar, hemp, flax, spruce canvas, and sail-cloth, with all manner of naval stores, which they generally have a consumption for in their own port, where they build a very great number of ships every year, besides refitting and repairing the old.

Add to this the coal trade between Newcastle and the river of Thames, in which they are so improved of late years that they have now a greater share of it than any other town in England, and have quite worked the Ipswich men out of it who had formerly the chief share of the colliery in their hands.

For the carrying on all these trades they must have a very great number of ships, either of their own or employed by them: and it may in some measure be judged of by this that in the year 1697, I had an account from the town register that there was then 1,123 sail of ships using the sea and belonged to the town, besides such ships as the merchants of Yarmouth might be concerned in, and be part owners of, belonging to any other ports.

To all this I must add, without compliment to the town or to the people, that the merchants, and even the generality of traders of Yarmouth, have a very good reputation in trade as well abroad as at home for men of fair and honourable dealing, punctual and just in their performing their engagements and in discharging commissions; and their seamen, as well masters as mariners, are justly esteemed among the ablest and most expert navigators in England.

This town, however populous and large, was ever contained in one parish, and had but one church; but within these two years they have built another very fine church near the south end of the town. The old church is dedicated to St. Nicholas, and was built by that famous Bishop of Norwich, William Herbert, who flourished in the reign of William II., and Henry I., William of Malmesbury, calls him Vir Pecuniosus; he might have called him Vir Pecuniosissimus, considering the times he lived in, and the works of charity and munificence which he has left as witnesses of his immense riches; for he built the Cathedral Church, the Priory for sixty monks, the Bishop's Palace, and the parish church of St. Leonard, all in Norwich; this great church at Yarmouth, the Church of St. Margaret at Lynn, and of St. Mary at Elmham. He removed the episcopal see from Thetford to Norwich, and instituted the Cluniack Monks at Thetford, and gave them or built them a house. This old church is very large, and has a high spire, which is a useful sea-mark.

Here is one of the finest market-places and the best served with provisions in England, London excepted; and the inhabitants are so multiplied in a few years that they seem to want room in their town rather than people to fill it, as I have observed above.

The streets are all exactly straight from north to south, with lanes or alleys, which they call rows, crossing them in straight lines also from east to west, so that it is the most regular built town in England, and seems to have been built all at once; or that the dimensions of the houses and extent of the streets were laid out by consent.

They have particular privileges in this town and a jurisdiction by which they can try, condemn, and execute in especial cases without waiting for a warrant from above; and this they exerted once very smartly in executing a captain of one of the king's ships of war in the reign of King Charles II. for a murder committed in the street, the circumstance of which did indeed call for justice; but some thought they would not have ventured to exert their powers as they did. However, I never heard that the Government resented it or blamed them for it.

It is also a very well-governed town, and I have nowhere in England observed the Sabbath day so exactly kept, or the breach so continually punished, as in this place, which I name to their honour.

Among all these regularities it is no wonder if we do not find abundance of revelling, or that there is little encouragement to assemblies, plays, and gaming meetings at Yarmouth as in some other places; and yet I do not see that the ladies here come behind any of the neighbouring counties, either in beauty, breeding, or behaviour; to which may be added too, not at all to their disadvantage, that they generally go beyond them in fortunes.

From Yarmouth I resolved to pursue my first design, viz., to view the seaside on this coast, which is particularly famous for being one of the most dangerous and most fatal to the sailors in all England—I may say in all Britain—and the more so because of the great number of ships which are continually going and coming this way in their passage between London and all the northern coasts of Great Britain. Matters of antiquity are not my inquiry, but principally observations on the present state of things, and, if possible, to give such accounts of things worthy of recording as have never been observed before; and this leads me the more directly to mention the commerce and the navigation when I come to towns upon the coast as what few writers have yet meddled with.

The reason of the dangers of this particular coast are found in the situation of the county and in the course of ships sailing this way, which I shall describe as well as I can thus:—The shore from the mouth of the River of Thames to Yarmouth Roads lies in a straight line from SSE. to NNW., the land being on the W. or larboard side.

From Wintertonness, which is the utmost northerly point of land in the county of Norfolk, and about four miles beyond Yarmouth, the shore falls off for nearly sixty miles to the west, as far as Lynn and Boston, till the shore of Lincolnshire tends north again for about sixty miles more as far as the Humber, whence the coast of Yorkshire, or Holderness, which is the east riding, shoots out again into the sea, to the Spurn and to Flamborough Head, as far east, almost, as the shore of Norfolk had given back at Winterton, making a very deep gulf or bay between those two points of Winterton and the Spurn Head; so that the ships going north are obliged to stretch away to sea from Wintertonness, and leaving the sight of land in that deep bay which I have mentioned, that reaches to Lynn and the shore of Lincolnshire, they go, I say, N. or still NNW. to meet the shore of Holderness, which I said runs out into the sea again at the Spurn; and the first land they make or desire to make, is called as above, Flamborough Head, so that Wintertonness and Flamborough Head are the two extremes of this course, there is, as I said, the Spurn Head indeed between; but as it lies too far in towards the Humber, they keep out to the north to avoid coming near it.

In like manner the ships which come from the north, leave the shore at Flamborough Head, and stretch away SSE. for Yarmouth Roads; and they first land they make is Wintertonness (as above). Now, the danger of the place is this: if the ships coming from the north are taken with a hard gale of wind from the SE., or from any point between NE. and SE., so that they cannot, as the seamen call it, weather Wintertonness, they are thereby kept within that deep bay; and if the wind blows hard, are often in danger of running on shore upon the rocks about Cromer, on the north coast of Norfolk, or stranding upon the flat shore between Cromer and Wells; all the relief they have, is good ground tackle to ride it out, which is very hard to do there, the sea coming very high upon them; or if they cannot ride it out then, to run into the bottom of the great bay I mentioned, to Lynn or Boston, which is a very difficult and desperate push: so that sometimes in this distress whole fleets have been lost here altogether.

The like is the danger to ships going northward, if after passing by Winterton they are taken short with a north-east wind, and cannot put back into the Roads, which very often happens, then they are driven upon the same coast, and embayed just as the latter. The danger on the north part of this bay is not the same, because if ships going or coming should be taken short on this side Flamborough, there is the river Humber open to them, and several good roads to have recourse to, as Burlington Bay, Grimsby Road, and the Spurn Head, and others, where they ride under shelter.

The dangers of this place being thus considered, it is no wonder, that upon the shore beyond Yarmouth there are no less than four lighthouses kept flaming every night, besides the lights at Castor, north of the town, and at Goulston S., all of which are to direct the sailors to keep a good offing in case of bad weather, and to prevent their running into Cromer Bay, which the seamen call the devil's throat.

As I went by land from Yarmouth northward, along the shore towards Cromer aforesaid, and was not then fully master of the reason of these things, I was surprised to see, in all the way from Winterton, that the farmers and country people had scarce a barn, or a shed, or a stable, nay, not the pales of their yards and gardens, not a hogstye, not a necessary house, but what was built of old planks, beams, wales, and timbers, etc., the wrecks of ships, and ruins of mariners' and merchants' fortunes; and in some places were whole yards filled and piled up very high with the same stuff laid up, as I supposed to sell for the like building purposes, as there should he occasion.

About the year 1692 (I think it was that year) there was a melancholy example of what I have said of this place: a fleet of 200 sail of light colliers (so they call the ships bound northward empty to fetch coals from Newcastle to London) went out of Yarmouth Roads with a fair wind, to pursue their voyage, and were taken short with a storm of wind at NE. after they were past Wintertonness, a few leagues; some of them, whose masters were a little more wary than the rest, or perhaps, who made a better judgment of things, or who were not so far out as the rest, tacked, and put back in time, and got safe into the roads; but the rest pushing on in hopes to keep out to sea, and weather it, were by the violence of the storm driven back, when they were too far embayed to weather Wintertonness as above, and so were forced to run west, everyone shifting for themselves as well as they could; some run away for Lynn Deeps, but few of them (the night being so dark) could find their way in there; some, but very few, rode it out at a distance; the rest, being above 140 sail, were all driven on shore and dashed to pieces, and very few of the people on board were saved: at the very same unhappy juncture, a fleet of laden ships were coming from the north, and being just crossing the same bay, were forcibly driven into it, not able to weather the Ness, and so were involved in the same ruin as the light fleet was; also some coasting vessels laden with corn from Lynn and Wells, and bound for Holland, were with the same unhappy luck just come out to begin their voyage, and some of them lay at anchor; these also met with the same misfortune, so that, in the whole, above 200 sail of ships, and above a thousand people, perished in the disaster of that one miserable night, very few escaping.

Cromer is a market town close to the shore of this dangerous coast. I know nothing it is famous for (besides it being thus the terror of the sailors) except good lobsters, which are taken on that coast in great numbers and carried to Norwich, and in such quantities sometimes too as to be conveyed by sea to London.

Farther within the land, and between this place and Norwich, are several good market towns, and innumerable villages, all diligently applying to the woollen manufacture, and the country is exceedingly fruitful and fertile, as well in corn as in pastures; particularly, which was very pleasant to see, the pheasants were in such great plenty as to be seen in the stubbles like cocks and hens—a testimony though, by the way, that the county had more tradesmen than gentlemen in it; indeed, this part is so entirely given up to industry, that what with the seafaring men on the one side, and the manufactures on the other, we saw no idle hands here, but every man busy on the main affair of life, that is to say, getting money; some of the principal of these towns are:—Alsham, North Walsham, South Walsham, Worsted, Caston, Reepham, Holt, Saxthorp, St. Faith's, Blikling, and many others. Near the last, Sir John Hobart, of an ancient family in this county, has a noble seat, but old built. This is that St. Faith's, where the drovers bring their black cattle to sell to the Norfolk graziers, as is observed above.

From Cromer we ride on the strand or open shore to Weyburn Hope, the shore so flat that in some places the tide ebbs out near two miles. From Weyburn west lies Clye, where there are large salt-works and very good salt made, which is sold all over the county, and sometimes sent to Holland and to the

Baltic. From Clye we go to Masham and to Wells, all towns on the coast, in each whereof there is a very considerable trade carried on with Holland for corn, which that part of the county is very full of. I say nothing of the great trade driven here from Holland, back again to England, because I take it to be a trade carried on with much less honesty than advantage, especially while the clandestine trade, or the art of smuggling was so much in practice: what it is now, is not to my present purpose.

Near this town lie The Seven Burnhams, as they are called, that is to say, seven small towns, all called by the same name, and each employed in the same trade of carrying corn to Holland, and bringing back,— etc.

From hence we turn to the south-west to Castle Rising, an old decayed borough town, with perhaps not ten families in it, which yet (to the scandal of our prescription right) sends two members to the British Parliament, being as many as the City of Norwich itself or any town in the kingdom, London excepted, can do.

On our left we see Walsingham, an ancient town, famous for the old ruins of a monastery of note there, and the Shrine of our Lady, as noted as that of St. Thomas-à-Becket at Canterbury, and for little else.

Near this place are the seats of the two allied families of the Lord Viscount Townsend and Robert Walpole, Esq.; the latter at this time one of the Lords Commissioners of the Treasury and Minister of State, and the former one of the principal Secretaries of State to King George, of which again.

From hence we went to Lynn, another rich and populous thriving port-town. It stands on more ground than the town of Yarmouth, and has, I think, parishes, yet I cannot allow that it has more people than Yarmouth, if so many. It is a beautiful, well built, and well situated town, at the mouth of the River Ouse, and has this particular attending it, which gives it a vast advantage in trade; namely, that there is the greatest extent of inland navigation here of any port in England, London excepted. The reason whereof is this, that there are more navigable rivers empty themselves here into the sea, including the washes, which are branches of the same port, than at any one mouth of waters in England, except the Thames and the Humber. By these navigable rivers, the merchants of Lynn supply about six counties wholly, and three counties in part, with their goods, especially wine and coals, viz., by the little Ouse, they send their goods to Brandon and Thetford, by the Lake to Mildenhall, Barton Mills, and St. Edmundsbury; by the River Grant to Cambridge, by the great Ouse itself to Ely, to St. Ives, to St. Neots, to Barford Bridge, and to Bedford; by the River Nyne to Peterborough; by the drains and washes to Wisbeach, to Spalding, Market Deeping, and Stamford; besides the several counties, into which these goods are carried by land-carriage, from the places, where the navigation of those rivers end; which has given rise to this observation on the town of Lynn, that they bring in more coals than any sea-port between London and Newcastle; and import more wines than any port in England, except London and Bristol; their trade to Norway and to the Baltic Sea is also great in proportion, and of late years they have extended their trade farther to the southward.

Here are more gentry, and consequently is more gaiety in this town than in Yarmouth, or even in Norwich itself—the place abounding in very good company.

The situation of this town renders it capable of being made very strong, and in the late wars it was so; a line of fortification being drawn round it at a distance from the walls; the ruins, or rather remains of which works appear very fair to this day; nor would it be a hard matter to restore the bastions, with the ravelins, and counterscarp, upon any sudden emergency, to a good state of defence: and that in a little time, a sufficient number of workmen being employed, especially because they are able to fill all their ditches with water from the sea, in such a manner as that it cannot be drawn off.

There is in the market-place of this town a very fine statue of King William on horseback, erected at the charge of the town. The Ouse is mighty large and deep, close to the very town itself, and ships of good burthen may come up to the quay; but there is no bridge, the stream being too strong and the bottom moorish and unsound; nor, for the same reason, is the anchorage computed the best in the world; but there are good roads farther down.

They pass over here in boats into the fen country, and over the famous washes into Lincolnshire, but the passage is very dangerous and uneasy, and where passengers often miscarry and are lost; but then it is usually on their venturing at improper times, and without the guides, which if they would be persuaded not to do, they would very rarely fail of going or coming safe.

From Lynn I bent my course to Downham, where is an ugly wooden bridge over the Ouse; from whence we passed the fen country to Wisbeach, but saw nothing that way to tempt our curiosity but deep roads, innumerable drains and dykes of water, all navigable, and a rich soil, the land bearing a vast quantity of good hemp, but a base unwholesome air; so we came back to Ely, whose cathedral, standing in a level flat country, is seen far and wide, and of which town, when the minster, so they call it, is described, everything remarkable is said that there is room to say. And of the minster, this is the most remarkable thing that I could hear it, namely, that some of it is so ancient, totters so much with every gust of wind, looks so like a decay, and seems so near it, that whenever it does fall, all that it is likely will be thought strange in it will be that it did not fall a hundred years sooner.

From hence we came over the Ouse, and in a few miles to Newmarket. In our way, near Snaybell, we saw a noble seat of the late Admiral Russell, now Earl of Orford, a name made famous by the glorious victory obtained under his command over the French fleet and the burning their ships at La Hogue—a victory equal in glory to, and infinitely more glorious to the English nation in particular, than that at Blenheim, and, above all, more to the particular advantage of the confederacy, because it so broke the heart of the naval power of France that they have not fully recovered it to this day. But of this victory it must be said it was owing to the haughty, rash, and insolent orders given by the King of France to his admiral, viz., to fight the confederate fleet wherever he found them, without leaving room for him to use due caution if he found them too strong, which pride of France was doubtless a fate upon them, and gave a cheap victory to the confederates, the French coming down rashly, and with the most impolitic bravery, with about five-and-forty sail to attack between seventy and eighty sail, by which means they met their ruin. Whereas, had their own fleet been joined, it might have cost more blood to have mastered them if it had been done at all.

The situation of this house is low, and on the edge of the fen country, but the building is very fine, the avenues noble, and the gardens perfectly finished. The apartments also are rich, and I see nothing wanting but a family and heirs to sustain the glory and inheritance of the illustrious ancestor who raised it—sed caret pedibus; these are wanting.

Being come to Newmarket in the month of October, I had the opportunity to see the horse races and a great concourse of the nobility and gentry, as well from London as from all parts of England, but they were all so intent, so eager, so busy upon the sharping part of the sport—their wagers and bets—that to me they seemed just as so many horse-coursers in Smithfield, descending (the greatest of them) from their high dignity and quality to picking one another's pockets, and biting one another as much as possible, and that with such eagerness as that it might be said they acted without respect to faith, honour, or good manners.

There was Mr. Frampton the oldest, and, as some say, the cunningest jockey in England; one day he lost one thousand guineas, the next he won two thousand; and so alternately he made as light of throwing away five hundred or one thousand pounds at a time as other men do of their pocket-money, and as perfectly calm, cheerful, and unconcerned when he had lost one thousand pounds as when he had won it. On the other side there was Sir R Fagg, of Sussex, of whom fame says he has the most in him and the least to show for it (relating to jockeyship) of any man there, yet he often carried the prize. His horses, they said, were all cheats, how honest soever their master was, for he scarce ever produced a horse but he looked like what he was not, and was what nobody could expect him to be. If he was as light as the wind, and could fly like a meteor, he was sure to look as clumsy, and as dirty, and as much like a cart-horse as all the cunning of his master and the grooms could make him, and just in this manner he beat some of the greatest gamesters in the field.

I was so sick of the jockeying part that I left the crowd about the posts and pleased myself with observing the horses: how the creatures yielded to all the arts and managements of their masters; how they took their airings in sport, and played with the daily heats which they ran over the course before the grand day. But how, as knowing the difference equally with their riders, would they exert their utmost strength at the time of the race itself! And that to such an extremity that one or two of them died in the stable when they came to be rubbed after the first heat.

Here I fancied myself in the Circus Maximus at Rome seeing the ancient games and the racings of the chariots and horsemen, and in this warmth of my imagination I pleased and diverted myself more and in a more noble manner than I could possibly do in the crowds of gentlemen at the weighing and starting-posts and at their coming in, or at their meetings at the coffee-houses and gaming-tables after the races were over, where there was little or nothing to be seen but what was the subject of just reproach to them and reproof from every wise man that looked upon them.

N.B.—Pray take it with you, as you go, you see no ladies at Newmarket, except a few of the neighbouring gentlemen's families, who come in their coaches on any particular day to see a race, and so go home again directly.

As I was pleasing myself with what was to be seen here, I went in the intervals of the sport to see the fine seats of the gentlemen in the neighbouring county, for this part of Suffolk, being an open champaign country and a healthy air, is formed for pleasure and all kinds of country diversion, Nature, as it were, inviting the gentlemen to visit her where she was fully prepared to receive them, in conformity to which kind summons they came, for the country is, as it were, covered with fine palaces of the nobility and pleasant seats of the gentlemen.

The Earl of Orford's house I have mentioned already; the next is Euston Hall, the seat of the Duke of Grafton. It lies in the open country towards the side of Norfolk, not far from Thetford, a place capable of all that is pleasant and delightful in Nature, and improved by art to every extreme that Nature is able to produce.

From thence I went to Rushbrook, formerly the seat of the noble family of Jermyns, lately Lord Dover, and now of the house of Davers. Here Nature, for the time I was there, drooped and veiled all the beauties of which she once boasted, the family being in tears and the house shut up, Sir Robert Davers, the head thereof, and knight of the shire for the county of Suffolk, and who had married the eldest daughter of the late Lord Dover, being just dead, and the corpse lying there in its funeral form of ceremony, not yet buried. Yet all looked lovely in their sorrow, and a numerous issue promising and grown up intimated that the family of Davers would still flourish, and that the beauties of Rushbrook, the mansion of the family, were not formed with so much art in vain or to die with the present possessor.

After this we saw Brently, the seat of the Earl of Dysert, and the ancient palace of my Lord Cornwallis, with several others of exquisite situation, and adorned with the beauties both of art and Nature, so that I think any traveller from abroad, who would desire to see how the English gentry live, and what pleasures they enjoy, should come into Suffolk and Cambridgeshire, and take but a light circuit among the country seats of the gentlemen on this side only, and they would be soon convinced that not France, no, not Italy itself, can outdo them in proportion to the climate they lived in.

I had still the county of Cambridge to visit to complete this tour of the eastern part of England, and of that I come now to speak.

We enter Cambridgeshire out of Suffolk, with all the advantage in the world; the county beginning upon those pleasant and agreeable plains called Newmarket Heath, where passing the Devil's Ditch, which has nothing worth notice but its name, and that but fabulous too, from the hills called Gogmagog, we see a rich and pleasant vale westward, covered with corn-fields, gentlemen's seats, villages, and at a distance, to crown all the rest, that ancient and truly famous town and university of Cambridge, capital of the county, and receiving its name from, if not, as some say, giving name to it; for if it be true that the town takes its name of Cambridge from its bridge over the river Cam, then certainly the shire or county, upon the division of England into counties, had its name from the town, and Cambridgeshire signifies no more or less than the county of which Cambridge is the capital town.

As my business is not to lay out the geographical situation of places, I say nothing of the buttings and boundings of this county. It lies on the edge of the great level, called by the people here the Fen Country; and great part, if not all, the Isle of Ely lies in this county and Norfolk. The rest of Cambridgeshire is almost wholly a corn country, and of that corn five parts in six of all they sow is barley, which is generally sold to Ware and Royston, and other great malting towns in Hertfordshire, and is the fund from whence that vast quantity of malt, called Hertfordshire malt, is made, which is esteemed the best in England. As Essex, Suffolk, and Norfolk are taken up in manufactures, and famed for industry, this county has no manufacture at all; nor are the poor, except the husbandmen, famed for anything so much as idleness and sloth, to their scandal be it spoken. What the reason of it is I know not.

It is scarce possible to talk of anything in Cambridgeshire but Cambridge itself; whether it be that the county has so little worth speaking of in it, or, that the town has so much, that I leave to others; however, as I am making modern observations, not writing history, I shall look into the county, as well as into the colleges, for what I have to say.

As I said, I first had a view of Cambridge from Gogmagog hills; I am to add that there appears on the mountain that goes by this name, an ancient camp or fortification, that lies on the top of the hill, with a double, or rather treble, rampart and ditch, which most of our writers say was neither Roman nor Saxon, but British. I am to add that King James II. caused a spacious stable to be built in the area of this camp for his running homes, and made old Mr. Frampton, whom I mentioned above, master or inspector of them. The stables remain still there, though they are not often made use of. As we descended westward we saw the Fen country on our right, almost all covered with water like a sea, the Michaelmas rains having been very great that year, they had sent down great floods of water from the upland countries, and those fens being, as may be very properly said, the sink of no less than thirteen counties—that is to say, that all the water, or most part of the water, of thirteen counties falls into them; they are often thus overflowed. The rivers which thus empty themselves into these fens, and which thus carry off the water, are the Cam or Grant, the Great Ouse and Little Ouse, the Nene, the Welland, and the river which runs from Bury to Milden Hall. The counties which these rivers drain, as above, are as follows:—

| | | |
|---|---|---|
| Lincoln | Warwick | Norfolk |
| Cambridge | Oxford | Suffolk |
| Huntingdon | Leicester | Essex |
| Bedford | Northampton | |
| Buckingham | Rutland | |

Those marked with (*) empty all their waters this way, the rest but in part.

In a word, all the water of the middle part of England which does not run into the Thames or the Trent, comes down into these fens.

In these fens are abundance of those admirable pieces of art called decoys that is to say, places so adapted for the harbour and shelter of wild fowl, and then furnished with a breed of those they call decoy ducks, who are taught to allure and entice their kind to the places they belong to, that it is incredible what quantities of wild fowl of all sorts, duck, mallard, teal, widgeon, &c., they take in those decoys every week during the season; it may, indeed, be guessed at a little by this, that there is a decoy not far from Ely which pays to the landlord, Sir Thomas Hare, £500 a year rent, besides the charge of maintaining a great number of servants for the management; and from which decoy alone, they assured me at St. Ives (a town on the Ouse, where the fowl they took was always brought to be sent to London) that they generally sent up three thousand couple a week.

There are more of these about Peterborough, who send the fowl up twice a week in waggon-loads at a time, whose waggons before the late Act of Parliament to regulate carriers I have seen drawn by ten and twelve horses a-piece, they were laden so heavy.

As these fens appear covered with water, so I observed, too, that they generally at this latter part of the year appear also covered with fogs, so that when the downs and higher grounds of the adjacent country were gilded with the beams of the sun, the Isle of Ely looked as if wrapped up in blankets, and nothing to be seen but now and then the lantern or cupola of Ely Minster.

One could hardly see this from the hills and not pity the many thousands of families that were bound to or confined in those fogs, and had no other breath to draw than what must be mixed with those vapours, and that steam which so universally overspreads the country. But notwithstanding this, the people, especially those that are used to it, live unconcerned, and as healthy as other folks, except now and then an ague, which they make light of, and there are great numbers of very ancient people among them.

I now draw near to Cambridge, to which I fancy I look as if I was afraid to come, having made so many circumlocutions beforehand; but I must yet make another digression before I enter the town (for in my way, and as I came in from Newmarket, about the beginning of September), I cannot omit, that I came necessarily through Stourbridge Fair, which was then in its height.

If it is a diversion worthy a book to treat of trifles, such as the gaiety of Bury Fair, it cannot be very unpleasant, especially to the trading part of the world, to say something of this fair, which is not only the greatest in the whole nation, but in the world; nor, if I may believe those who have seen the mall, is the fair at Leipzig in Saxony, the mart at Frankfort-on-the-Main, or the fairs at Nuremberg, or Augsburg, any way to compare to this fair at Stourbridge.

It is kept in a large corn-field, near Casterton, extending from the side of the river Cam, towards the road, for about half a mile square.

If the husbandmen who rent the land, do not get their corn off before a certain day in August, the fair-keepers may trample it under foot and spoil it to build their booths, or tents, for all the fair is kept in tents and booths. On the other hand, to balance that severity, if the fair-keepers have not done their business of the fair, and removed and cleared the field by another certain day in September, the ploughmen may come in again, with plough and cart, and overthrow all, and trample into the dirt; and as for the filth, dung, straw, etc. necessarily left by the fair-keepers, the quantity of which is very great, it is the farmers' fees, and makes them full amends for the trampling, riding, and carting upon, and hardening the ground.

It is impossible to describe all the parts and circumstances of this fair exactly; the shops are placed in rows like streets, whereof one is called Cheapside; and here, as in several other streets, are all sorts of trades, who sell by retail, and who come principally from London with their goods; scarce any trades are omitted—goldsmiths, toyshops, brasiers, turners, milliners, haberdashers, hatters, mercers, drapers, pewterers, china-warehouses, and in a word all trades that can be named in London; with coffee-houses, taverns, brandy-shops, and eating-houses, innumerable, and all in tents, and booths, as above.

This great street reaches from the road, which as I said goes from Cambridge to Newmarket, turning short out of it to the right towards the river, and holds in a line near half a mile quite down to the river-side: in another street parallel with the road are like rows of booths, but larger, and more intermingled with wholesale dealers; and one side, passing out of this last street to the left hand, is a formal great square, formed by the largest booths, built in that form, and which they call the Duddery; whence the name is derived, and what its signification is, I could never yet learn, though I made all possible search into it. The area of this square is about 80 to 100 yards, where the dealers have room before every booth to take down, and open their packs, and to bring in waggons to load and unload.

This place is separated, and peculiar to the wholesale dealers in the woollen manufacture. Here the booths or tents are of a vast extent, have different apartments, and the quantities of goods they bring are so great, that the insides of them look like another Blackwell Hall, being as vast warehouses piled up with goods to the top. In this Duddery, as I have been informed, there have been sold one hundred thousand pounds worth of woollen manufactures in less than a week's time, besides the prodigious trade carried on here, by wholesale men, from London, and all parts of England, who transact their business wholly in their pocket-books, and meeting their chapmen from all parts, make up their accounts, receive money chiefly in bills, and take orders: These they say exceed by far the sales of goods actually brought to the fair, and delivered in kind; it being frequent for the London wholesale men to carry back orders from their dealers for ten thousand pounds' worth of goods a man, and some much more. This especially respects those people, who deal in heavy goods, as wholesale grocers, salters, brasiers, iron-merchants, wine-merchants, and the like; but does not exclude the dealers in woollen manufactures, and especially in mercery goods of all sorts, the dealers in which generally manage their business in this manner.

Here are clothiers from Halifax, Leeds, Wakefield and Huddersfield in Yorkshire, and from Rochdale, Bury, etc., in Lancashire, with vast quantities of Yorkshire cloths, kerseys, pennistons, cottons, etc., with all sorts of Manchester ware, fustians, and things made of cotton wool; of which the quantity is so great, that they told me there were near a thousand horse-packs of such goods from that side of the country, and these took up a side and half of the Duddery at least; also a part of a street of booths were taken up with upholsterer's ware, such as tickings, sackings, kidderminster stuffs, blankets, rugs, quilts, etc.

In the Duddery I saw one warehouse, or booth with six apartments in it, all belonging to a dealer in Norwich stuffs only, and who, they said, had there above twenty thousand pounds value in those goods, and no other.

Western goods had their share here also, and several booths were filled as full with serges, duroys, druggets, shalloons, cantaloons, Devonshire kerseys, etc., from Exeter, Taunton, Bristol, and other parts west, and some from London also.

But all this is still outdone at least in show, by two articles, which are the peculiars of this fair, and do not begin till the other part of the fair, that is to say for the woollen manufacture begins to draw to a close. These are the wool and the hops; as for the hops, there is scarce any price fixed for hops in England, till they know how they sell at Stourbridge fair; the quantity that appears in the fair is indeed prodigious, and they, as it were, possess a large part of the field on which the fair is kept to themselves; they are brought directly from Chelmsford in Essex, from Canterbury and Maidstone in Kent, and from Farnham in Surrey, besides what are brought from London, the growth of those and other places.

Enquiring why this fair should be thus, of all other places in England, the centre of that trade; and so great a quantity of so bulky a commodity be carried thither so far; I was answered by one thoroughly acquainted with that matter thus: the hops, said he, for this part of England, grow principally in the two counties of Surrey and Kent, with an exception only to the town of Chelmsford in Essex, and there are very few planted anywhere else.

There are indeed in the west of England some quantities growing: as at Wilton, near Salisbury; at Hereford and Broomsgrove, near Wales, and the like; but the quantity is inconsiderable, and the places remote, so that none of them come to London.

As to the north of England, they formerly used but few hops there, their drink being chiefly pale smooth ale, which required no hops, and consequently they planted no hops in all that part of England, north of the Trent; nor did I ever see one acre of hop-ground planted beyond Trent in my observation; but as for some years past, they not only brew great quantities of beer in the north, but also use hops in the brewing their ale much more than they did before; so they all come south of Trent to buy their hops; and here being quantities brought, it is great part of their back carriage into Yorkshire, and Northamptonshire, Derbyshire, Lancashire, and all these counties; nay, of late, since the Union, even to Scotland itself; for I must not omit here also to mention, that the river Grant, or Cam, which runs close by the north-west side of the fair in its way from Cambridge to Ely, is navigable, and that by this means, all heavy goods are brought even to the fair-field, by water carriage from London and other parts; first to the port of Lynn, and then in barges up the Ouse, from the Ouse into the Cam, and so, as I say, to the very edge of the fair.

In like manner great quantities of heavy goods, and the hops among the rest, are sent from the fair to Lynn by water, and shipped there for the Humber, to Hull, York, etc., and for Newcastle-upon-Tyne, and by Newcastle, even to Scotland itself. Now as there is still no planting of hops in the north, though a great consumption, and the consumption increasing daily, this, says my friend, is one reason why at Stourbridge fair there is so great a demand for the hops. He added, that besides this, there were very few hops, if any worth naming, growing in all the counties even on this side Trent, which were above forty miles from London; those counties depending on Stourbridge fair for their supply, so the counties of Suffolk, Norfolk, Cambridge, Huntingdon, Northampton, Lincoln, Leicester, Rutland, and even to Stafford, Warwick, and Worcestershire, bought most if not all of their hops at Stourbridge fair.

These are the reasons why so great a quantity of hops are seen at this fair, as that it is incredible, considering, too, how remote from this fair the growth of them is as above.

This is likewise a testimony of the prodigious resort of the trading people of all parts of England to this fair; the quantity of hops that have been sold at one of these fairs is diversely reported, and some affirm it to be so great, that I dare not copy after them; but without doubt it is a surprising account, especially in a cheap year.

The next article brought thither is wool, and this of several sorts, but principally fleece wool, out of Lincolnshire, where the longest staple is found; the sheep of those countries being of the largest breed.

The buyers of this wool are chiefly indeed the manufacturers of Norfolk and Suffolk and Essex, and it is a prodigious quantity they buy.

Here I saw what I have not observed in any other county of England, namely, a pocket of wool. This seems to be first called so in mockery, this pocket being so big, that it loads a whole waggon, and reaches beyond the most extreme parts of it hanging over both before and behind, and these ordinarily weigh a ton or twenty-five hundredweight of wool, all in one bag.

The quantity of wool only, which has been sold at this place at one fair, has been said to amount to fifty or sixty thousand pounds in value, some say a great deal more.

By these articles a stranger may make some guess at the immense trade carried on at this place; what prodigious quantities of goods are bought and sold here, and what a confluence of people are seen here from all parts of England.

I might go on here to speak of several other sorts of English manufactures which are brought hither to be sold; as all sorts of wrought-iron and brass-ware from Birmingham; edged tools, knives, etc., from Sheffield; glass wares and stockings from Nottingham and Leicester; and an infinite throng of other things of smaller value every morning.

To attend this fair, and the prodigious conflux of people which come to it, there are sometimes no less than fifty hackney coaches which come from London, and ply night and morning to carry the people to and from Cambridge; for there the gross of the people lodge; nay, which is still more strange, there are wherries brought from London on waggons to ply upon the little river Cam, and to row people up and down from the town, and from the fair as occasion presents.

It is not to be wondered at, if the town of Cambridge cannot receive, or entertain the numbers of people that come to this fair; not Cambridge only, but all the towns round are full; nay, the very barns and stables are turned into inns, and made as fit as they can to lodge the meaner sort of people: as for the people in the fair, they all universally eat, drink, and sleep in their booths and tents; and the said booths are so intermingled with taverns, coffee-houses, drinking-houses, eating-houses, cook-shops, etc., and all in tents too; and so many butchers and higglers from all the neighbouring counties come into the fair every morning with beef, mutton, fowls, butter, bread, cheese, eggs, and such things, and go with them from tent to tent, from door to door, that there is no want of any provisions of any kind, either dressed or undressed.

In a word, the fair is like a well-fortified city, and there is the least disorder and confusion I believe, that can be seen anywhere with so great a concourse of people.

Towards the latter end of the fair, and when the great hurry of wholesale business begins to be over, the gentry come in from all parts of the county round; and though they come for their diversion, yet it is not a little money they lay out, which generally falls to the share of the retailers, such as toy-shops, goldsmiths, braziers, ironmongers, turners, milliners, mercers, etc., and some loose coins they reserve for the puppet shows, drolls, rope-dancers, and such like, of which there is no want, though not considerable like the rest. The last day of the fair is the horse-fair, where the whole is closed with both horse and foot races, to divert the meaner sort of people only, for nothing considerable is offered of that kind. Thus ends the whole fair, and in less than a week more, there is scarce any sign left that there has been such a thing there, except by the heaps of dung and straw and other rubbish which is left behind, trod into the earth, and which is as good as a summer's fallow for dunging the land; and as I have said above, pays the husbandman well for the use of it.

I should have mentioned that here is a court of justice always open, and held every day in a shed built on purpose in the fair; this is for keeping the peace, and deciding controversies in matters deriving from the business of the fair. The magistrates of the town of Cambridge are judges in this court, as being in their jurisdiction, or they holding it by special privilege: here they determine matters in a summary way, as is practised in those we call Pye Powder Courts in other places, or as a Court of Conscience; and they have a final authority without appeal.

I come now to the town and university of Cambridge; I say the town and university, for though they are blended together in the situation, and the colleges, halls, and houses for literature are promiscuously scattered up and down among the other parts, and some even among the meanest of the other buildings, as Magdalene College over the bridge is in particular; yet they are all incorporated together by the name of the university, and are governed apart and distinct from the town which they are so intermixed with.

As their authority is distinct from the town, so are their privileges, customs, and government; they choose representatives, or members of Parliament for themselves, and the town does the like for themselves, also apart.

The town is governed by a mayor and aldermen; the university by a chancellor, and vice-chancellor, etc. Though their dwellings are mixed, and seem a little confused, their authority is not so; in some cases the vice-chancellor may concern himself in the town, as in searching houses for the scholars at improper hours, removing scandalous women, and the like.

But as the colleges are many, and the gentlemen entertained in them are a very great number, the trade of the town very much depends upon them, and the tradesmen may justly be said to get their bread by the colleges; and this is the surest hold the university may be said to have of the townsmen, and by which they secure the dependence of the town upon them, and consequently their submission.

I remember some years ago a brewer, who being very rich and popular in the town, and one of their magistrates, had in several things so much opposed the university, and insulted their vice-chancellor, or other heads of houses, that in short the university having no other way to exert themselves, and show their resentment, they made a bye-law or order among themselves, that for the future they would not trade with him; and that none of the colleges, halls, etc., would take any more beer of him; and what followed? The man indeed braved it out a while, but when he found he could not obtain a revocation of the order, he was fain to leave off his brewhouse, and if I remember right, quitted the town.

Thus I say, interest gives them authority; and there are abundance of reasons why the town should not disoblige the university, as there are some also on the other hand, why the university should not differ to any extremity with the town; nor, such is their prudence, do they let any disputes between them run up to any extremities if they can avoid it. As for society; to any man who is a lover of learning, or of learned men, here is the most agreeable under heaven; nor is there any want of mirth and good company of other kinds; but it is to the honour of the university to say, that the governors so well understand their office, and the governed their duty, that here is very little encouragement given to those seminaries of crime, the assemblies, which are so much boasted of in other places.

Again, as dancing, gaming, intriguing are the three principal articles which recommend those assemblies; and that generally the time for carrying on affairs of this kind is the night, and sometimes all night, a time as unseasonable as scandalous; add to this, that the orders of the university admit no such excesses; I therefore say, as this is the case, it is to the honour of the whole body of the university that no encouragement is given to them here.

As to the antiquity of the university in this town, the originals and founders of the several colleges, their revenues, laws, government, and governors, they are so effectually and so largely treated of by other authors, and are so foreign to the familiar design of these letters, that I refer my readers to Mr. Camden's "Britannia" and the author of the "Antiquities of Cambridge," and other such learned writers, by whom they may be fully informed.

The present Vice-Chancellor is Dr. Snape, formerly Master of Eaton School near Windsor, and famous for his dispute with, and evident advantage over, the late Bishop of Bangor in the time of his government; the dispute between the University and the Master of Trinity College has been brought to a head so as to employ the pens of the learned on both sides, but at last prosecuted in a judicial way so as to deprive Dr. Bentley of all his dignities and offices in the university; but the doctor flying to the royal protection, the university is under a writ of mandamus, to show cause why they do not restore the doctor again, to which it seems they demur, and that demur has not, that we hear, been argued, at least when these sheets were sent to the press. What will be the issue time must show.

From Cambridge the road lies north-west on the edge of the fens to Huntingdon, where it joins the great north road. On this side it is all an agreeable corn country as above, adorned with several seats of gentlemen; but the chief is the noble house, seat, or mansion of Wimple or Wimple Hall, formerly built at a vast expense by the late Earl of Radnor, adorned with all the natural beauties of situation, and to which was added all the most exquisite contrivances which the best heads could invent to make it artificially as well as naturally pleasant.

However, the fate of the Radnor family so directing, it was bought with the whole estate about it by the late Duke of Newcastle, in a partition of whose immense estate it fell to the Right Honourable the Lord Harley, son and heir-apparent of the present Earl of Oxford and Mortimer, in right of the Lady Harriet Cavendish, only daughter of the said Duke of Newcastle, who is married to his lordship, and brought him this estate and many other, sufficient to denominate her the richest heiress in Great Britain.

Here his lordship resides, and has already so recommended himself to this county as to be by a great majority chosen Knight of the Shire for the county of Cambridge.

From Cambridge, my design obliging me, and the direct road in part concurring, I came back through the west part of the county of Essex, and at Saffron Walden I saw the ruins of the once largest and most magnificent pile in all this part of England—viz., Audley End—built by, and decaying with, the noble Dukes and Earls of Suffolk.

A little north of this part of the country rises the River Stour, which for a course of fifty miles or more parts the two counties of Suffolk and Essex, passing through or near Haveril, Clare, Cavendish, Halsted, Sudbury, Bowers, Nayland, Stretford, Dedham, Manningtree, and into the sea at Harwich, assisting by its waters to make one of the best harbours for shipping that is in Great Britain—I mean Orwell Haven or Harwich, of which I have spoken largely already.

As we came on this side we saw at a distance Braintree and Bocking, two towns, large, rich, and populous, and made so originally by the bay trade, of which I have spoken at large at Colchester, and which flourishes still among them.

The manor of Braintree I found descended by purchase to the name of Olmeus, the son of a London merchant of the same name, making good what I had observed before, of the great number of such who have purchased estates in this county.

Near this town is Felsted, a small place, but noted for a free school of an ancient foundation, for many years under the mastership of the late Rev. Mr. Lydiat, and brought by him to the meridian of its reputation. It is now supplied, and that very worthily, by the Rev. Mr. Hutchins.

Near to this is the Priory of Lees, a delicious seat of the late Dukes of Manchester, but sold by the present Duke to the Duchess Dowager of Bucks, his Grace the Duke of Manchester removing to his yet finer seat of Kimbolton in Northamptonshire, the ancient mansion of the family. From hence keeping the London Road I came to Chelmsford, mentioned before, and Ingerstone, five miles west, which I mention again, because in the parish church of this town are to be seen the ancient monuments of the noble family of Petre, whose seat and large estate lie in the neighbourhood, and whose whole family, by a constant series of beneficent actions to the poor, and bounty upon all charitable occasions, have gained an affectionate esteem through all that part of the country such as no prejudice of religion could wear out, or perhaps ever may; and I must confess, I think, need not, for good and great actions command our respect, let the opinions of the persons be otherwise what they will.

From hence we crossed the country to the great forest, called Epping Forest, reaching almost to London. The country on that side of Essex is called the Roodings, I suppose, because there are no less than ten towns almost together, called by the name of Roding, and is famous for good land, good malt, and dirty roads; the latter indeed in the winter are scarce passable for horse or man. In the midst of this we see Chipping Onger, Hatfield Broad Oak, Epping, and many forest towns, famed as I have said for husbandry and good malt, but of no other note. On the south side of the county is Waltham Abbey; the ruins of the abbey remain, and though antiquity is not my proper business, I could not but observe that King Harold, slain in the great battle in Sussex against William the Conqueror, lies buried here; his body being begged by his mother, the Conqueror allowed it to be carried hither; but no monument was, as I can find, built for him, only a flat gravestone, on which was engraven Harold Infelix.

From hence I came over the forest again—that is to say, over the lower or western part of it, where it is spangled with fine villages, and these villages filled with fine seats, most of them built by the citizens of London, as I observed before, but the lustre of them seems to be entirely swallowed up in the magnificent palace of the Lord Castlemain, whose father, Sir Josiah Child, as it were, prepared it in his life for the design of his son, though altogether unforeseen, by adding to the advantage of its situation innumerable rows of trees, planted in curious order for avenues and vistas to the house, all leading up to the place where the old house stood, as to a centre.

In the place adjoining, his lordship, while he was yet Sir Richard Child only, and some years before he began the foundation of his new house, laid out the most delicious, as well as most spacious, pieces of ground for gardens that is to be seen in all this part of England. The greenhouse is an excellent building, fit to entertain a prince; it is furnished with stoves and artificial places for heat from an apartment in which is a bagnio and other conveniences, which render it both useful and pleasant. And these gardens have been so the just admiration of the world, that it has been the general diversion of the citizens to go out to see them, till the crowds grew too great, and his lordship was obliged to restrain his servants from showing them, except on one or two days in a week only.

The house is built since these gardens have been finished. The building is all of Portland stone in the front, which makes it look extremely glorious and magnificent at a distance, it being the particular property of that stone (except in the streets of London, where it is tainted and tinged with the smoke of the city) to grow whiter and whiter the longer it stands in the open air.

As the front of the house opens to a long row of trees, reaching to the great road at Leightonstone, so the back face, or front (if that be proper), respects the gardens, and, with an easy descent, lands you upon the terrace, from whence is a most beautiful prospect to the river, which is all formed into canals and openings to answer the views from above and beyond the river; the walks and wildernesses go on to such a distance, and in such a manner up the hill, as they before went down, that the sight is lost in the woods adjoining, and it looks all like one planted garden as far as the eye can see.

I shall cover as much as possible the melancholy part of a story which touches too sensibly many, if not most, of the great and flourishing families in England. Pity and matter of grief is it to think that families, by estate able to appear in such a glorious posture as this, should ever be vulnerable by so mean a disaster as that of stock-jobbing. But the general infatuation of the day is a plea for it, so that men are not now blamed on that account. South Sea was a general possession, and if my Lord Castlemain was wounded by that arrow shot in the dark it was a misfortune. But it is so much a happiness that it was not a mortal wound, as it was to some men who once seemed as much out of the reach of it. And that blow, be it what it will, is not remembered for joy of the escape, for we see this noble family, by prudence and management, rise out of all that cloud, if it may be allowed such a name, and shining in the same full lustre as before.

This cannot be said of some other families in this county, whose fine parks and new-built palaces are fallen under forfeitures and alienations by the misfortunes of the times and by the ruin of their masters' fortunes in that South Sea deluge.

But I desire to throw a veil over these things as they come in my way; it is enough that we write upon them, as was written upon King Harold's tomb at Waltham Abbey, Infelix, and let all the rest sleep among things that are the fittest to be forgotten.

From my Lord Castlemain's, house and the rest of the fine dwellings on that side of the forest, for there are several very good houses at Wanstead, only that they seem all swallowed up in the lustre of his lordship's palace, I say, from thence, I went south, towards the great road over that part of the forest called the Flats, where we see a very beautiful but retired and rural seat of Mr. Lethulier's, eldest son of the late Sir John Lethulier, of Lusum, in Kent, of whose family I shall speak when I come on that side.

By this turn I came necessarily on to Stratford, where I set out. And thus having finished my first circuit, I conclude my first letter, and am,

Sir, your most humble
and obedient servant.


APPENDIX.

Whoever travels, as I do, over England, and writes the account of his observations, will, as I noted before, always leave something, altering or undertaking by such a growing improving nation as this, or something to discover in a nation where so much is hid, sufficient to employ the pens of those that come after him, or to add by way of appendix to what he has already observed.

This is my case with respect to the particulars which follow: (1) Since these sheets were in the press, a noble palace of Mr. Walpole's, at present First Commissioner of the Treasury, Privy-counsellor, etc., to King George, is, as it were, risen out of the ruins of the ancient seat of the family of Walpole, at Houghton, about eight miles distant from Lynn, and on the north coast of Norfolk, near the sea.

As the house is not yet finished, and when I passed by it was but newly designed, it cannot be expected that I should be able to give a particular description of what it will be. I can do little more than mention that it appears already to be exceedingly magnificent, and suitable to the genius of the great founder.

But a friend of mine, who lives in that county, has sent me the following lines, which, as he says, are to be placed upon the building, whether on the frieze of the cornice, or over the portico, or on what part of the building, of that I am not as yet certain. The inscription is as follows, viz.:—

"H. M. P.

"Fundamen ut essem Domûs

In Agro Natali Extruendæ,
Robertus ille Walpole
Quem nulla nesciet Posteritas:

Faxit Dues.

"Postquam Maturus Annis Dominus.
Diu Lætatus fuerit absolutâ
Incolumem tueantur Incolames.
Ad Summam omnium Diem
Et nati natorum et qui nascentur ab illis.

Hic me Posuit."

A second thing proper to be added here, by way of appendix, relates to what I have mentioned of the Port of London, being bounded by the Naze on the Essex shore, and the North Foreland on the Kentish shore, which some people, guided by the present usage of the Custom House, may pretend is not so, to answer such objectors. The true state of that case stands thus:

"(1) The clause taken from the Act of Parliament establishing the extent of the Port of London, and published in some of the books of rates, is this:

"'To prevent all future differences and disputes touching the extent and limits of the Port of London, the said port is declared to extend, and be accounted from the promontory or point called the North Foreland in the Isle of Thanet, and from thence northward in a right line to the point called the Naze, beyond the Gunfleet upon the coast of Essex, and so continued westward throughout the river Thames, and the several channels, streams, and rivers falling into it, to London Bridge, saving the usual and known rights, liberties, and privileges of the ports of Sandwich and Ipswich, and either of them, and the known members thereof, and of the customers, comptrollers, searchers, and their deputies, of and within the said ports of Sandwich and Ipswich and the several creeks, harbours, and havens to them, or either of them, respectively belonging, within the counties of Kent and Essex.'

"II. Notwithstanding what is above written, the Port of London, as in use since the said order, is understood to reach no farther than Gravesend in Kent and Tilbury Point in Essex, and the ports of Rochester, Milton, and Faversham belong to the port of Sandwich.

"In like manner the ports of Harwich, Colchester, Wivenhoe, Malden, Leigh, etc., are said to be members of the port of Ipswich."

This observation may suffice for what is needful to be said upon the same subject when I may come to speak of the port of Sandwich and its members and their privileges with respect to Rochester, Milton, Faversham, etc., in my circuit through the county of Kent.

Daniel Defoe – A Short Biography

Daniel Foe was born around 1660 in Fore Street in the parish of St. Giles Cripplegate in London.

The aristocratic-sounding 'De' was added to his name to create 'Defoe'. On occasion he was prone to claim descent from the family of De Beau Faux.

His father, James Foe, was a prosperous tallow chandler and a member of the Worshipful Company of Butchers and, with Defoe's mother, Annie, Presbyterian dissenters.

Defoe has been born into a time that was rich in dramatic history. In 1665, 70,000 were killed by the Great Plague of London. The following year the Great Fire of London destroyed much of mediaeval London. The Defoe house was one of the few to survive.

In 1667, a third calamity beset London when a Dutch fleet sailed up the Medway via the River Thames and attacked the town of Chatham, as well as destroying much of the British fleet.

By the time Defoe was aged ten accounts suggest his mother, Annie, had died.

Defoe's education began at James Fisher's boarding school in Pixham Lane in Dorking, Surrey. By 14 he was attending a dissenting academy at Newington Green in London run by Charles Morton, and he is then believed to have attended the Newington Green Unitarian Church. During this period, the English government persecuted those who chose to worship outside the Church of England.

Defoe entered the world of business as a general merchant, dealing at different times in hosiery, general woollen goods and wine. His ambitions were great and he was able to buy a country estate, a ship as well as civets, though he was rarely out of debt. (The civet produces an odorous secretion for the purpose of marking out their territory. Diluted, after some time, the odor of civet secretion, normally strong and repulsive, becomes pleasant with animalistic-musk nuance. The animals are kept in cages in order to be able to collect the secretions and thence perfume).

In 1684, Defoe married Mary Tuffley, the daughter of a London merchant, and received a dowry of £3,700 – a huge amount by the standards of the day. With his debts and political difficulties, the marriage may have been troubled, but it lasted 50 years.

In 1685, Defoe joined the ill-fated Monmouth Rebellion but gained a pardon, by which he escaped the Bloody Assizes of the notorious Judge George Jeffreys.

The Glorious Revolution brought Queen Mary and her husband William III to the crown in 1688, and Defoe became one of William's close allies and a secret agent. Some of the new Government policies led to conflict with France, thus damaging many of Defoe's trade relationships.

In 1692, Defoe was arrested for debts of £700 and his civets were taken away. His actual debts are thought to have been nearer £17,000. His laments were loud and he always sided with debtors, but there is evidence that his financial dealings were always above board.

With a wife and seven children to support it was essential that his release was quickly enabled. He achieved this and accounts then suggest he travelled to Europe and Scotland, perhaps to re-establish some business relationships and to trade wine.

By 1695, he was back in England, serving as a "commissioner of the glass duty", and responsible for collecting the tax on bottles. The following year, 1696, he ran a tile and brick factory in what is now Tilbury in Essex and the family lived in the parish of Chadwell St Mary.

Defoe's first notable publication was not one of his great fiction works but a series of proposals for social and economic improvements, a subject for which he had a keen eye and many ideas. An Essay upon Projects was published in 1697.

His most successful poem, The True-Born Englishman (1701), defended the king against the perceived xenophobia of his enemies, satirising the English claim to racial purity. That same year Defoe presented the Legion's Memorial to the Speaker of the House of Commons and later his employer, Robert Harley, flanked by a guard of sixteen gentlemen of quality. It demanded the release of the Kentish petitioners, who had asked Parliament to support the king in an imminent war against France.

In 1702 the death of William III once more created a political crisis. Queen Anne immediately began an attack against Non-conformists. Defoe was one of the first targets. His pamphleteering and political activities quickly resulted in his arrest. This seemed mainly predicated on his December 1702 pamphlet; The Shortest-Way with the Dissenters; Or, Proposals for the Establishment of the Church, which argued for their extermination. In it, he ruthlessly satirised both the High church Tories and those Dissenters who hypocritically practised so-called "occasional conformity". Although it was published anonymously, the Defoe's authorship was quickly unmasked and he was arrested and charged with seditious libel. In fact, Defoe's ironic writing had been misinterpreted, but, alas for him, his trial was to be at the Old bailey in front of the sadistic judge Salathiel Lovell.

Lovell sentenced him to a punitive fine of 200 marks, to public humiliation in a pillory at Charing Cross and an indeterminate length of imprisonment at the Queen's pleasure which would cease only on payment of the enormous fine.

This was an awful moment for Defoe. After his three days in the pillory, he was imprisoned at Newgate.

In despair, he wrote to William Paterson, the London Scot and founder of the Bank of England and who was in the confidence of Robert Harley, 1st Earl of Oxford and Earl Mortimer, a leading minister and spymaster in the English Government. Harley arranged Defoe's release, in 1703, in exchange for Defoe's co-operation as an intelligence agent for the Tories. In exchange for such co-operation with the rival political side, Harley paid some of Defoe's very large outstanding debts, which greatly improved his financial situation.

With his release from Newgate Defoe had, within a few days, witnessed the Great Storm of November 26th, 1703. It caused immense damage to an area from London to Bristol, uprooting millions of trees, and claiming the lives of over 8,000 people, mostly at sea. This became the subject of The Storm (1704), which included many eye-witness accounts and is regarded as one of the world's first examples of modern journalism.

In the same year, he set up his periodical A Review of the Affairs of France which supported the Harley Ministry, and chronicled the events of the War of the Spanish Succession (1702–1714). The Review initially ran weekly but was soon being printed three times a week. Defoe wrote most of the articles himself and although in effect the Review was a Government publication Defoe was enthusiastic and energetic as ever.

Harley was ousted from the ministry in 1708, but Defoe continued writing the Review to support a new master, Godolphin, then again to support Harley and his return in the Tory ministry of 1710–1714. The Tories fell from power with the death of Queen Anne, but Defoe continued his work, now for the Whig government, writing 'Tory' pamphlets that undermined the Tory point of view.

Not all of Defoe's pamphlet writing was political. One pamphlet was originally published anonymously, entitled 'A True Relation of the Apparition of One Mrs. Veal the Next Day after her Death to One Mrs. Bargrave at Canterbury the 8th of September, 1705.' It deals with the crossover between the spiritual and physical realms and describes Mrs. Bargrave's encounter with her old friend Mrs. Veal after she had died.

In 1709, Defoe authored a rather lengthy book entitled The History of the Union of Great Britain. The book attempts to explain the facts leading up to the Act of Union 1707, dating all the way back to December 6th, 1604 when King James was presented with a proposal for unification. (It should be remembered that since the death of Queen Elizabeth England and Scotland, although separate kingdoms, had a common monarch; known as James I of England and as James VI of Scotland. The act now brought the two countries into one; Great Britain.

Part of Defoe's duties as a Government spokesman and spy was the relaying of the Governments view to the public. He thought that his work on the Review would end the threat from the north and gain for the Treasury an "inexhaustible treasury of men", a valuable new market increasing the power of England, clearly the senior partner in the Union. In September 1706, Harley ordered Defoe to Edinburgh to do everything he could to secure loyalty to the Treaty of Union. Defoe was conscious of the risk he was taking. His reports were often vivid descriptions of violent demonstrations against the Union. "A Scots rabble is the worst of its kind", he reported.

Defoe was a Presbyterian who had suffered in England for his convictions, and as such he was accepted as an adviser to the General Assembly of the Church of Scotland and committees of the Parliament of Scotland with little problem.

Defoe received little in the way of reward or recognition from his pay-masters or the government. However, like any good writer, the experiences would be filed away for later use. The Scottish experience was helpful when he came to write his Tour Thro' the Whole Island of Great Britain, published in 1726.

Defoe continued to keep up a wide and varied output including in his apologia Appeal to Honour and Justice (1715), a defence of his part in Harley's Tory ministry (1710–14), The Family Instructor (1715), a conduct manual on religious duty; Minutes of the Negotiations of Monsr. Mesnager (1717), in which he impersonates Nicolas Mesnager, who negotiated the Treaty of Utrecht (1713); and A Continuation of the Letters Writ by a Turkish Spy (1718), a satire of European politics and religion, written by Defoe in the guise of a Muslim in Paris.

From this point Defoe would now enter a period of writing that would cement his place in the canon of English fiction. From 1719 to 1724, Defoe published the novels for which he is now world-famous including Robinson Crusoe in 1719 and Moll Flanders in 1724 amongst many others.

In the final decade of his life, he also wrote conduct manuals, including Religious Courtship (1722), The Complete English Tradesman (1726) and The New Family Instructor (1727).

Defoe seemed to have a natural knack of writing across a wide range of subjects and from a number of points of view. He published on the breakdown of the social order; The Great Law of Subordination Considered (1724) and Everybody's Business is Nobody's Business (1725), together with works on the supernatural; The Political History of the Devil (1726), A System of Magick (1727) and An Essay on the History and Reality of Apparitions (1727). His works on foreign travel and trade include A General History of Discoveries and Improvements (1727) and Atlas Maritimus and Commercialis (1728). Perhaps his greatest achievement is the magisterial A Tour Thro' the Whole Island of Great Britain (1724–27), which provided a panoramic survey of British trade on the eve of the Industrial Revolution.

Published in 1726, The Complete English Tradesman is a late example of Defoe's political and social work. He discusses the role of the tradesman in England in comparison to those abroad, arguing that the British system of trade is far superior. He also states that trade is the backbone of the British economy: "estate's a pond, but trade's a spring."

Defoe was obviously keenly aware of both political and economic structures. Trade, Defoe argues, is a much better vehicle for social and economic change than war. He states that through imperialism and trade expansion the British empire is able to "increase commerce at home" through job creation and increased consumption. This increased consumption, by laws of supply and demand, increases production which in turn raises wages for the poor therefore lifting part of British society further out of poverty.

Daniel Defoe died on April 24th, 1731. Some accounts say that it was whilst hiding from his creditors. Indeed, Defoe was known to enjoy walking on a Sunday when, legally, it was the only day of the week when he could not be legally pestered about his bills. The cause of his death was given as lethargy, but it is thought it was more probably a stroke.

He was interred in Bunhill Fields, London. A monument was erected to his memory there in 1870.

There are various suggestions as to the number of works in Defoe's literary output. Certainly, no less than 200 separate pieces but accounts suggest perhaps as many as 500 which seems, even for so prolific a writer as Defoe, rather too generous but perhaps is in keeping with the extravagance of his life.

Daniel Defoe – A Concise Bibliography

Defoe wrote an immense amount of works. Some were under pseudonyms or anonymously and others may merely have been attributed to him. The list below is by no means exhaustive but is certainly illustrative of both his range and scope.

Novels
Robinson Crusoe (1719)
The Farther Adventures of Robinson Crusoe (1719)
Serious Reflections During the Life and Surprising Adventures of Robinson Crusoe; With His Vision of the Angelic World (1720)

Captain Singleton (1720)
Memoirs of a Cavalier (1720)
A Journal of the Plague Year (1722)
Colonel Jack (1722)
Moll Flanders (1722)
Roxana: The Fortunate Mistress (1724)
Memoirs of a Cavalier: A Military Journal of the Wars in Germany, and the Wars in England.: From the Year 1632 to the Year 1648 (1724)
A New Voyage Round the World (1725)
Military Memoirs of Capt. George Carleton (1728)
A General History of the Pyrates, From their First Rise and Settlement in the Island of Providence, to the Present Time (1724)
The History of the Pyrates (1728)
Of Captain Misson and his Crew (1728)


Essays, Satires & Other Pieces
An Essay Upon Projects (1697)
The Shortest Way with the Dissenters (1702)
New Test of Church of England's Loyalty (1702)
Ode to the Athenian Society (1703)
Enquiry into Acgill's General Translation (1703)
The Storm– a description of the worst storm to hit Britain in recorded times, which includes eyewitness accounts. (1704)
The Great Law of Subordination Consider'd (1704)
Layman's Sermon on the Late Storm (1704)
Elegy on Author of 'True–Born Englishman,' (1704)
Hymn to Victory (1704)
An Essay on the Regulation of the Press (1704)
Giving Alms No Charity (1704)
The Consolidator or, Memoirs of Sundry Transactions from the World in the Moon (1705)
A True Relation of the Apparition of Mrs. Veal (1706)
Sermon on the Filling-up of Dr. Burgess's Meeting-house (1706)
History of the Union of Great Britain (1709)
Atalantis Major (1711)
A Short narrative of the Life and Actions of His Grace John, Duke of Marlborough (1711)
A Seasonable Warning and Caution Against the Insinuations of Papists and Jacobites in Favour of the Pretender (1712)
Short Enquiry into a Late Duel (1713)
A General History of Trade (1713)
An Answer to a Question That Nobody Thinks of, VIZ. But What if the Queen should die? (1713)
Reasons Against the Succession of the House of Hanover with an Enquiry How far the Abdication of King James, Supposing it to be Legal, Ought to Affect the Person of the Pretender (1713)
Wars of Charles III. (1715)
The Family Instructor (1715)
Hymn to the Mob (1715)
The Family Instructor (1715)

An Appeal to Honour and Justice, Though It Be of His Worst Enemies: Being A True Account of His Conduct in Public Affairs (1715)
A Friendly Epistle by Way of Reproof from one of the People Called Quakers, to T. B., a Dealer in Many Words (1715)
Memoirs of the Church of Scotland (1717)
Life and Death of Count Patkul (1717)
Memoirs of the Church of Scotland (1717)
Memoirs of Major Alexander Ramkins (1718)
Memoirs of Duke of Shrewsbury (1718)
Memoirs of Daniel Williams (1718)
A Vindication of the Press (1718)
Dickory Cronke: The Dumb Philosopher: or, Great Britain's Wonder (1719)
The King of Pirates (Capt. Avery) (1719)
Life of Baron de Goertz (1719)
Life and Adventures of Duncan Campbell (1720)
Mr. Campbell's Pacquet (1720)
The Supernatural Philosopher; or, The Mysteries of Magick (1720)
Due Preparations for the Plague (1722)
Life of Cartouche (1722)
Religious Courtship (1722)
History of Peter the Great (1723)
The Highland Rogue (Rob Roy) (1723)
Narrative of Murders at Calais (1724)
The History of The Remarkable Life of John Sheppard (1724)
A Narrative of All The Robberies, Escapes, &c. of John Sheppard (1724)
A Tour Thro' the Whole Island of Great Britain, Divided into Circuits or Journies (1724–1727)
The Great Law of Subordination; or, the Insolence and Insufferable Behaviour of Servants in England (1724)
Account of Jonathan Wild (1725)
Account of John Gow (1725)
Every-body's Business, Is No-body's Business (1725)
The Complete English Tradesman (1725; volume II, 1727)
The Friendly Demon (1726)
Mere Nature Delineated (Peter the Wild Boy) (1726)
Essay upon Literature and the Original of Letters (1726)
History of Discoveries (1726–7)
A System of Magic (1726)
The Protestant Monastery (1726)
The Political History of the Devil (1726)
An Essay Upon Literature (1726)
Mere Nature Delineated (1726)
Conjugal Lewdness (1727)
Treatise concerning Use and Abuse of Marriage (1727)
Secrets of Invisible World Discovered; or, History and Reality of Apparitions (1727)
Parochial Tyranny (1727)
A New Family Instructor (1728)
Augusta Triumphans: or, The Way to Make London the Most Flourishing City in the Universe (1728)
Plan of English Commerce (1728)

Second Thoughts are Best (on Street Robberies) (1728)
Street Robberies Considered (1728)
A Plan of the English Commerce (1728)
Humble Proposal to People of England for Increase of Trade, &c. (1729)
Preface to R. Dodsley's Poem 'Servitude' (1729)
Effectual Scheme for Preventing Street Robberies (1731)

Works in Verse
A New Discovery of an Old Intreague (1691)
Character of Dr. Samuel Annesley (1697)
The Pacificator (1700)
The True-Born Englishman: A Satyr (1701)
Reformation of Manners (1702)
The Mock Mourners (1702)
More Reformation (1703)
Hymn to the Pillory (1703)
The Dyet of Poland (1705)
Jure Divino. A Satyr in 12 books. (1706)
Caledonia (1706)
Translation of Du Fresnoy's "Compleat Art of Painting" (1720)

www.ingramcontent.com/pod-product-compliance
Lightning Source LLC
Chambersburg PA
CBHW061248040426
42444CB00010B/2290